AQA Art and Design

GCSE

Mike Ager

Frank Barnes

Martin Piercy

Anne Stewart

Series editor

Peter Dryland

Nelson Thornes

Published in 2009 by:
Nelson Thornes Ltd
Delta Place
27 Bath Road
CHELTENHAM
GL53 7TH
United Kingdom

10 11 12 13 / 10 9 8 7 6 5 4 3 2

A catalogue record for this book is available from the British Library

ISBN 978 1 4085 0320 1

Cover photograph by Will Howells
Picture research by Kay Altwegg
Page make-up by Fakenham Photosetting

Printed in China by 1010 Printing International Ltd

Acknowledgements

The authors and publishers wish to thank the following for permission to use copyright material:

1.7 (both images) The Estate of Francis Bacon. All rights reserved. DACS 2009/Dublin City Gallery Hugh Lane, 1.8 The Estate of Francis Bacon. All rights reserved. DACS 2009/Private Collection/Lauros/Giraudon/The Bridgeman Art Library, 1.14 ADAGP, Paris and DACS, London 2009/The Art Archive, 1.27 Musee Marmottan, Paris, France/Giraudon/The Bridgeman Art Library, 1.29 Estate of Robert Rauschenberg/DACS, London/VAGA, New York 2009/akg-images, 1.32 The Art Archive, 1.33 Musee des Arts Decoratifs, Paris, France/Lauros/Giraudon/The Bridgeman Art Library, 1.34 (top) Folio 3v from Quoderni di Anatornia vol. 2, Leonardo de Vinci 1499 (pen and ink on paper). Private Collection/The Bridgeman Art Library and (bottom) Alamy, 1.35 MATT BROWN ART, 1.37 DACS 2009/ The Bridgeman Art Library, 1.39 Kate Malone, Big Boy Gourd Vase 2005. Crystaline-glazed stoneware, height 50cm diameter 31cm www.adriansassoon.com, 1.41 Art Institute of Chicago, IL, USA/The Bridgeman Art Library.

2.18 Sue Lawty, Six Stone Sketchbook Pages, 2004. Natural stone on paper, each 15 x 11cm/Jerry Hardman-Jones, 2.21 and 2.22 Andy Goldsworthy, from WOOD by Andy Goldsworthy, 2.28 Barbara Kruger.

3.1 2009 Banco de Mexico Diego Rivera & Frida Kahlo Museums Trust, Mexico D.F./DACS/photo © Christie's Images The Bridgeman Art Library, 3.2 Reproduced by permission of the Henry Moore Foundation/The Bridgeman Art Library, 3.16 ADAGP, Paris and DACS, London 2009/The Art Archive, 3.27 Bill Brandt Archive Ltd, 3.28 Ernst Haas/Hulton Archive/Getty Images, 3.34 Succession Picasso/ DACS 2009/Tate Images, 3.49 Adobe product screenshot reprinted with permission of Adobe Systems Incorporated, 3.54 ADAGP, PARIS and DACS, London 2009/Tate Images, 3.56 Copyright Estate of Eileen Agar/Tate Images, 3.58 Estate of Robert Rauschenberg/ DACS, London/VAGA, New York 2009/Smithsonion American Art Museum, Washington, DC/Art Resource, New York, 3.60 Peter Blake. All rights reserved, DACS 2009/Tate Images.

4.15 and 4.16 www.jimrobison.co.uk, 4.20 Alamy, 4.24 Rijksmuseum, Amsterdam, The Netherlands/The Bridgeman Art Library, 4.25 Geoffrey Clements/Corbis, 4.31 Estate of Robert Rauschenberg/DACS, London/VAGA, New York 2009/The Bridgeman Art Library.

Contents

Nelson Thornes and AQA

Nelson Thornes has worked in partnership with AQA to ensure this book and the accompanying online resources offer you the best support for your GCSE course.

All resources have been approved by senior AQA examiners so you can feel assured that they closely match the specification for this subject and provide you with everything you need to prepare successfully for your exams.

These print and online resources together **unlock blended learning**; this means that the links between the case studies in the book and the case studies online blend together to maximise your understanding of the assessment objectives and help you achieve your potential.

These online resources are available on *kerboodle!* which can be accessed via the internet at **www.kerboodle.com/live**, anytime, anywhere. If your school or college subscribes to *kerboodle!* you will be provided with your own personal login details. Once logged in, access your course and locate the required resource.

For more information and help on how to use *kerboodle!* visit **www.kerboodle.com**.

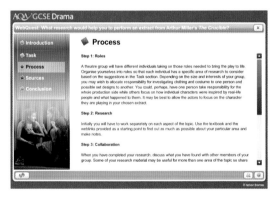

How to use this book

Objectives

Look for the list of **Learning Objectives** based on the requirements of this course so you can ensure you are covering everything you need to know.

AQA Examiner's tip

Don't forget to read the **AQA Examiner's Tips** throughout the book.

Visit **www.nelsonthornes.com/aqagcse** for more information.

About this book

This student handbook is designed to help you to get the most out of your new GCSE course in Art and Design and to ensure that you fulfil the necessary assessment objectives in both the controlled assessment (portfolio) unit and in the exam (externally set task) unit. It will also help you to improve your chances of success in both units by providing you with inspiring examples and ideas to help you to make informed choices in your own work. It is not a revision guide, like the ones produced to prepare you for exams in other subjects. This student handbook is designed to be used throughout the course, alongside the taught programme provided by your teachers and tutors in schools and colleges.

In GCSE Art and Design, courses are designed to provide you with many creative, exciting and stimulating opportunities. This book will help you to understand the course requirements, and it will offer you ideas that you might wish to consider, with illustrated examples of project work produced by GCSE students like yourself. Remember that these are just some of the many ways that students work, and that they are examples and suggestions, not required ways of working that you must follow. Also included are useful references to artwork produced by a range of artists, craftspeople and designers. Some may have explored similar themes that link with the student projects, whilst others have been selected to show unusual or exciting ways of working that might be of interest to you.

You have chosen to study Art and Design at GCSE level. The course will provide you with progression from your Key Stage 3 courses, and it will also prepare you if you wish to continue to study Art and Design in the future. This handbook takes you through the four areas of the course (known as the Assessment Objectives) that you will be required to cover. These are: Developing ideas; Using resources, media and materials; Recording ideas and observations and Making a personal, informed and meaningful response. The order that they are presented in the handbook is not necessarily the order in which you have to work; you will also notice that these areas all interrelate. You can dip into the chapters to find out information, to look for ideas and to support the work that you are developing at school or college.

The controlled assessment (portfolio of work) and externally set tasks in this book are examples of student's work and are designed to support your studies. The work you submit to AQA for assessment must be your own work and you cannot use the examples of work displayed in this book as your own. Your teacher can only give you general guidance for your controlled assessment and examination work.

About the course

Under the title of Art and Design, there are a number of options. You will be studying one or more from the list below. The handbook covers samples of work taken from all of the endorsements to exemplify different ways of working. They are:

1 Art and Design (full or short course)
2 Art and Design – Applied
3 Art and Design – Fine Art
4 Art and Design – Graphic Communication
5 Art and Design – Textile Design
6 Art and Design – Three-Dimensional Design
7 Art and Design – Photography: lens-based and light-based media

Each endorsement offers a wealth of possibilities for you to produce practical and critical/contextual work using a wide variety and combination of materials, processes and technologies, much of which can be seen in the handbook. The main difference between entry for the Art and Design course (full or short course) and one of the endorsements is in the content of what you produce. The endorsed courses focus on either project briefs that are vocational in nature (as in the case of the Applied course), or on specific areas related to that endorsement (such as illustration, advertising, packaging and multimedia etc. as in the case of Graphic Communication). Art and Design is a broad course in which you are expected to cover work from two or more of the endorsements. During the course you might, for example, experience a Textile Design project relating to fashion and costume; you might create a ceramic form within a Three-Dimensional Design project and you could explore the variety of ways to apply paint as part of a Fine Art project.

Projects

Your portfolio, which in total will include projects, assignments and/ or collections of work, needs to show that you have covered all four Assessment Objectives. If you study a full course in any of the Art and Design endorsements, you will be required to include more than one project (assignment or extended collection of work) within your coursework portfolio submission. Examples of these are shown in the handbook to help you to understand how the work fulfils the assessment objectives. If you study for the Short Course in Art and Design, you will be expected to include one project (assignment or extended collection of work) in your portfolio submission.

What does this mean in real terms? A project is a way of working through an artistic journey, taking an idea from a starting point to a realised outcome. A project usually covers all four assessment objectives, so there must be evidence that you can develop ideas through research and investigations and that you can select and experiment with appropriate resources, materials, processes and techniques. There must be evidence of recording ideas and observations, which might be through drawing, taking photographs, making notes, creating maquettes and models, or producing design sheets, as well as some sort of realised outcome. You may be given a title or a theme by your teacher/

tutor that the whole group will work on, or you may be given the opportunity to develop your own theme or title. The type of project you do might relate to an issue; it could be based on a cultural or historical theme; it might be a design brief; it could be based around using certain materials, or it might be a theme such as 'still life' or 'portraits' – in fact the possibilities are endless.

◼ Assessment

The course itself is divided into two areas for assessment:

- ▪ Unit 1: Portfolio of Work. This is marked out of 80 and carries 60% of your total marks.
- ▪ Unit 2: Externally Set Task. This is also marked out of 80 and carries 40% of your total marks.

◼ The portfolio

This is the coursework element of your GCSE course which is also known as "Controlled Assessment". It refers to the work that you develop during the course, and there is no restriction on the scale or type of work produced. Most of the work that you do will be produced in the classroom or studio under the guidance of your teacher/tutor, and it will reflect the wide variety of activities you experience during the taught programme. You must be able to confirm anything produced outside lessons as your own work, not that of anyone else. The content of the portfolio will vary from student to student and from endorsement to endorsement. As well as the projects that you undertake, there may be opportunities to attend workshops, visit galleries and museums, work with artists in residence and work collaboratively in groups. All of this evidence can be included in the portfolio, but it is not necessary to put in everything that you do during the course. In consultation with your teacher/tutor, you should carefully select, organise and present your work for the portfolio.

◼ The externally set task

This is the examination element of the course. You will receive an examination paper with a number of alternative starting points that are

written specifically for your endorsement. Textile Design candidates, for example, will have a different paper to those taking Graphic Communication, but the same paper is used for those taking the full and short course in Art and Design. Students taking the Applied endorsement will receive an examination paper containing a project scenario and a number of design briefs to choose from. You will need to select **one** starting point. A period of preparation time will be followed by ten hours of examination sessions in which you will work unaided to complete your response to your chosen starting point.

Helpful hints for success

▪ Familiarise yourself with the assessment objectives – by doing this at the start of the course, you will understand what is expected of you and how you can gain marks.

▪ Work to the best of your ability right from the beginning – a positive approach and a determination to succeed is essential.

▪ Keep a record of what you do – this might be by way of a sketch book, journal, log, ideas book, photo journal, electronic database or working diary, and will ensure that you can show evidence of your work as it progresses.

▪ Practise regularly – whether this is in drawing from primary sources or using a sewing machine; taking successful photographs or working in clay; mixing colours or using a range of computer programs.

▪ Allow yourself time to do the work effectively – nothing can be achieved easily, so allow yourself adequate time to achieve what you want, both in class and outside lessons.

▪ Learn from your mistakes – this is a very important element in the course. Every experience is worthwhile in art and design because you can then move forward to the next step.

▪ Learn from others – including your teachers and peers as well as a range of selected sources such as contemporary, historical and cultural practitioners.

▪ Develop good habits – by respecting your work and taking responsibility for your own success, you will have greater ownership of it.

▪ Keep your eyes open to the visual world around you – look at familiar things with a fresh approach, see how aspects of art and design make up your world and be aware of what affect these have on you and others.

▪ Be open to ideas and suggestions – do not close your mind to things that may appear unfamiliar or difficult to understand as sometimes these can be the most exciting experiences in art and design when you explore them further.

▪ Be confident in what you do – believe in yourself and remember that there are lots of ways to do things, all of which are as valuable as each other.

Your questions answered

What is the difference between the Full Course and the Short Course in Art and Design?

The Short Course is worth half a Full Course GCSE. The difference is in the amount of work that you will submit in Unit 1 (Portfolio of Work). In the Short Course, you are expected to select work that includes **one** project or extended collection of work. For the Full Course, **more than one** project or an extended collection of work is required. You must cover all four Assessment Objectives in the Portfolio. For Unit 2, the Externally Set Task, the same question paper is used for both the Full and Short courses, concluding with 10 hours of examination time to produce your own unaided personal response.

Can I take the Full Course in one year or does it have to be a two year course?

It is possible to take any full course endorsement in one year. You must, however, fulfil the criteria required for the four Assessment Objectives, submitting approximately 45 hours of selected work for the Portfolio (Unit 1), and ensuring that you have adequate preparatory time prior to completing the 10-hour Externally Set Task (Unit 2).

After I finish the 10 hours of exam time can I go back to my preparatory studies and do more work?

No, this is not possible because the final session of the ten hour exam signifies the end of Unit 2. You can, however, return to the Portfolio (Unit 1) to add more work or to select and refine pieces in that unit.

What is meant by a 'portfolio'?

A 'portfolio' in this context is another word for a collection of coursework. It can include work of any scale, so it does not have to fit into a designated size of folder. It can include work in any medium, such as drawing and painting; large scale 3D installations; digital, video or lens-based work; responses to visits and workshops; client based designs for specific briefs; experimental and developmental work as well as finished pieces; research into sources such as the work of artists, craftspeople and designers; sketch books as well as mounted work – in fact anything that reflects the breadth of the course that you have taken.

How much coursework do I need to do for a full GCSE qualification?

For a full course, your portfolio must cover all four of the assessment objectives and contain more than one project that shows sustained work from a starting point to your chosen outcome.

Do I have to work in a sketchbook?

For many students, working in a sketchbook is favourable because everything is in one place. It can be carried around easily and can be used for quick sketches, collecting samples and ideas, recording media experiments and research. The sketchbook often becomes a work of art in itself. Other students prefer to work in different ways and the choice is yours.

Can I enter for more than one GCSE in Art and Design?

There are no prohibited combinations of endorsements. If you take more than one course, it is important that there is no overlap of content between the areas of study. You cannot submit the same work for two different endorsements and you will take an Externally Set Task for each one.

Do I have to research the work of others in every project?

By familiarising yourself with and learning from selected sources you can extend your ideas and work. This may be through investigating the techniques and processes used by contemporary artists, designers and craftspeople, or by researching work from the past. By understanding the cultural, social and historical context of a piece of work, you will be able to connect with the meaning and purpose of it. Some of the projects that you are set will link directly to an art movement, period of history, culture or a source such as a film, book, performance or piece of music, but other work that you do may not relate to critical or cultural references. Because your Portfolio materials are marked holistically (i.e. all of the work is marked together) it is not necessary to research the work of others in every project or task, but it must be included in Unit 1 as a whole. It must be included in

Unit 2 as well. Always indicate your sources when referring to the work of others.

Do I have to produce a final piece for every project?

You can "present a personal, informed and meaningful response" and "realise intentions" in many different ways. This may not mean that you have to have a fully realised final outcome, but it is important to achieve what you set out to do. That might be a finished piece, or it might be a design proposal to present to a client, or it could be a collection of samples or trials with particular materials.

Do I have to write down lots of information?

You **will not** be disadvantaged if you do not include written work in your submission. If you decide to annotate your work, ensure that what you write is appropriate and that it supports what you are doing. The quality of any extended piece or pieces of writing will be assessed in AO3, and you can have guidance from your teacher/tutor with spelling and grammar during the course as you would in any other subject.

If I take the Photography endorsement do I have to use a dark room or can I work digitally?

It is perfectly acceptable to use traditional processes or digital photography, or if you wish you can use a combination of both traditional and new technologies. It is important, though, that if your work is presented as an electronic file for marking, it is clearly labelled and shows how you have selected, developed, reviewed and refined your initial images.

If I take the Applied course, do I have to work with a real client?

The Applied endorsement, being vocational in nature, requires you to work on project briefs that are client-orientated where you might be given a budget to work within or constraints of materials and size to keep to. This does not mean that you must always work with 'real' clients in a genuine work place, but you must have experience of professional practice in order to understand how design proposals are presented to clients.

Who decides what projects I have to study?

Tasks or projects will usually be provided by your teachers/tutors, but you may be given the opportunity to select and develop your own starting points. It is only in the Externally Set Task that the project starting points are set by the examination board.

Who will mark my work?

Initially your work will be marked by your own teachers/tutors and their marks will then be moderated by a representative of the examination board to check that standards are maintained.

1 Developing ideas

Objectives

In this chapter you will learn how to:

select a starting point

resource your ideas

develop ideas

use contextual and other sources

demonstrate analytical and cultural understanding.

Everyone has ideas. They are stimulated by experiences, the senses, memories and imagination. In Art and Design you should develop your ideas through investigations that are informed by **contextual and other sources**, refine ideas through experimenting with materials and techniques, and by recording your thoughts, observations and insights to enable you to realise your intentions. They will take on greater depth and meaning as you develop your analytical skills and cultural understanding.

1.1 *Study in oil paint*

1.2 *Ideas expressed in Graphic Communication*

1.3 *Thumbnail sketch capturing movement*

1.4 *Mixed media study*

Approaches to the development of ideas

Selecting a starting point

Generating ideas from a **starting point** can happen in a number of ways. They may spring from your response to a theme, an idea, an issue or a brief, from collecting materials and objects, from information gathered during a visit to a gallery or museum, or from the experience of a workshop or fieldtrip. Ideas can reflect your own personality and experiences.

Your class might be provided with a single starting point, a theme or a **design brief** by your art teacher or you might be given a number of starting points to choose from. You might be given the opportunity to write your own brief. In the Externally Set Task, Unit 2, you will be able to select from a number of starting points. Before you decide on a starting point, ask yourself:

- Will your choice keep your interest?
- Will it make best use of your abilities and strengths?
- Will it help you to develop your skills and understanding?
- Are suitable **source materials** available?

During the early stages of your investigations you might be attracted to more than one starting point.

You could make preliminary investigations into a few different starting points, to help you decide which one to pursue towards an outcome. However, don't waste time; if working on more than one starting point be decisive about which has the most potential.

Alternative approaches

You do not have to start a project with work from observation: your ideas could develop from looking at other artists', designers' or craftspersons' work, or by experimenting with materials.

Key terms

Contextual sources: examples of art, craft and design, cultural objects, artefacts, including architecture from different times and cultures.

Starting point: a theme, object, issue or brief.

Design brief: developing ideas with a defined focus, particularly in Graphic Communication, Three-Dimensional Design, Textile Design and Applied Art.

Source materials: materials such as objects, artefacts and images from which you develop your work and ideas. They might include texts, poetry, writing, sound, music, TV and film.

AQA Examiner's tip

Notes and annotations, where appropriate, can sometimes help to clarify your ideas and explain them to others.

Case study 1

Selecting a starting point in Fine Art

Lauren is a GCSE Fine Art student who responded to the theme of 'Environments' in the Externally Set Task, Unit 2, by looking at Impressionist landscapes. Influenced by the effects of light on water she had seen in some of the Impressionists' work, she took a series of photographs on location, and selected six of her images that she thought had the potential for further investigation (Figure 1.5). Her intention was to develop ideas for compositions, lighting effects and colour combinations similar to those she had seen in Impressionist paintings. Recording from primary sources meant that Lauren was able to alter her viewpoint and frame her subject. For example, she deliberately included foliage in the foreground while framing the composition in Figure 1.5, and returned to a beach on different days and times in order to capture the changing light and weather effects.

Lauren analysed her images and selected four of them to investigate, using paint to produce studies (Figure 1.6) from her photographs. Through this process, Lauren was able to select the idea she considered to have the greatest potential for development.

Remember

You might have to account for things like time, travel costs and admission fees when planning to work on location.

Alternative approaches

Lauren could have developed her ideas differently by focusing on the techniques used by Georges Seurat, or by digitally manipulating her photographs of landscapes.

1.5 *Lauren's six selected photographs*

1.6 *Painted sketches from photographs*

Resourcing your ideas

Collecting suitable source material is important in the development of ideas, and should be done in a selective and discriminating way. The material that you collect can take many forms, depending on the nature of the starting point, but you need to ensure that what you collect is relevant to your intentions.

Resourcing ideas and identifying **source material** to work from might involve investigating magazines, books, printed and electronic media, or result from fieldwork, a visit to a museum or an art gallery. You might make sketches and drawings, or take photographs in a particular location. Perhaps you have the opportunity to work with artists, craftspeople or designers in their studios, or in workshops or artists' residencies set up in your school or college. Remember that the material you find and collect needs to be relevant and selected thoughtfully.

Gathering material can involve a number of research activities, including visual, written, oral or other means:

- collecting objects, specimens or materials
- collecting images
- making drawings
- using a camera

■ making a video or sound recording

■ making notes.

Source materials

Source material might be gathered from your immediate surroundings, your home or classroom for example, from an environment or location that you have visited or from other sources. It should include contextual material which might be in the form of works by other artists, craftspeople and designers, or artefacts and other material from different cultures and different times. You might choose to select source material such as a film, television programme, poem, a piece of text or music, or an issue or event, from which to develop your ideas.

Material can be gathered from primary and secondary sources. Working directly from your source material allows you to experience objects and places, using all your senses to inform your response. Not only can you see the material but you might also touch, smell and, perhaps, hear it. Images of a busy market or station might be less vivid without having the experience of the sounds and smells that contribute to their atmosphere. If, for example, you are working directly from the human figure or objects you can easily change your viewpoint. If you are analysing contextual material such as a painting, you could look at it close-up and from further away. First-hand, you could walk around a sculpture or explore a ceramic piece or packaging design from different angles.

Secondary sources can often spark ideas as well as providing source materials that otherwise might not be available to you. Photographs and images from magazines, books and other printed sources, and from the internet, are a rich and valuable resource. These sources can give you access to examples of art, crafts and design from different places and times, but also they can provide images that document people's lives, different cultures, events in history and in the modern world.

◯◯ links

Primary and secondary sources are discussed in more detail at the beginning of Chapter 3.

AQA *Examiner's tip*

Be sure to acknowledge the origins of any source material that is not your own.

◯◯ links

Most museums and galleries have their own websites. Good links can be found at:

www.artinfo.com

See also:

http.//artchive.com

www.artcyclopedia.com

www.nationalgallery.org.uk

www.tate.org.uk

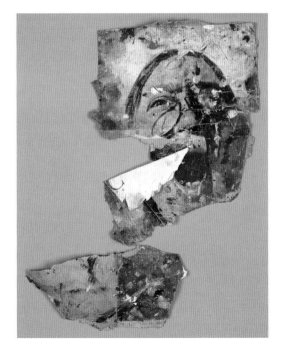

1.7 *Source material found in Francis Bacon's studio*

1.8 *Francis Bacon* Study after Velazquez's Portrait of Pope Innocent X *(1953)*

Case study 2

Working with source material in Art and Design

Kathryn investigated sources to support her study into the theme of 'Memories'. From both primary and secondary sources she collected objects, artefacts and images which had a particular importance to her; photographs of family and friends, cuttings from newspapers, pressed flowers, pieces of jewellery, and so on.

Kathryn set out to create a distinctive mood of faded, misty, half-forgotten memories of things, people, clothing and conversations, expressed in a way that was very personal to her. She developed a working method using mixed media and collage, where words, images and objects were of equal importance, but also where the visual elements become tangled, overlapped and layered (Figure 1.9). By integrating her carefully selected source material into her work, the materials she collected became part of the work itself.

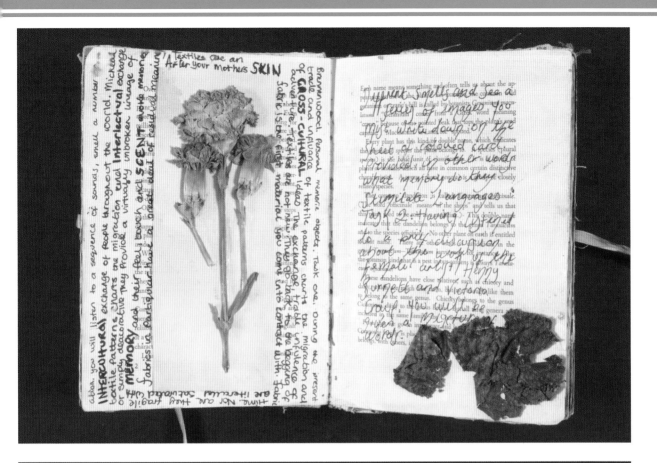

1.9   *Two double page spreads of ideas from Kathryn's sketchbook incorporating some of her source materials*

kerboodle!

Your source material might include:

- natural or manufactured objects
- the natural or built environment
- the human form
- images
- sound recordings
- texts, poetry, performance, film or music
- issues-based material
- textured or patterned surfaces
- lettering styles
- materials from different belief systems or cultures.

⃝⃝links

See Chapter 3 on recording ideas for ways to show evidence of how to communicate your thinking.

Starting to develop ideas

Once you have identified and obtained your source materials you can investigate them and begin to develop your ideas. You will probably have some ideas when you choose a starting point or as you look for source material, but these initial ideas might be quite vague. Development of your ideas can only really begin through the process of investigation of your source materials, including contextual sources, and through experimentation with media, processes and techniques.

You might work from primary or secondary sources, or a combination of both. If, for example, you were responding to the theme of architecture, you might take photographs of buildings, or make a series of drawings of architectural details. You might choose to focus on decoration or construction, old buildings or modern buildings. You might collect items of builders' or surveyors' equipment, plans, blueprints or pieces of building materials. You might investigate books or the internet for examples of interesting or unusual buildings, or the work of a particular architect.

Experimenting with different media and interpreting your source materials using different techniques and approaches can often lead to results that are not predictable. Part of the excitement of the 'journey' of investigation is to make unexpected discoveries that become the trigger for developing your ideas in ways that you could not have predicted when you began.

> **Remember**
>
> Check the availability and appropriateness of your source material.

⃝⃝links

See Chapter 2 for ideas on selecting and experimenting with appropriate resources, media, techniques and processes.

Case study 3

Developing ideas in Three-Dimensional Design

Josh is taking the Art and Design endorsement and he investigated the theme of 'The Body' for a Three-Dimensional Design project as part of his Unit 1 Portfolio of Work. He was particularly interested in the internal workings of the body, and his ideas were developed from studies of veins, nerves and blood vessels. The nature of his work meant that his research was sourced entirely from secondary sources in the form of medical illustrations and diagrams from books and the internet.

Josh decided that he would concentrate on the idea of two blood vessels twisting together (Figure 1.10). The development of his own ideas was informed by some of the colourful organic forms based on viruses, atoms and body parts produced by the ceramicist Kate Malone.

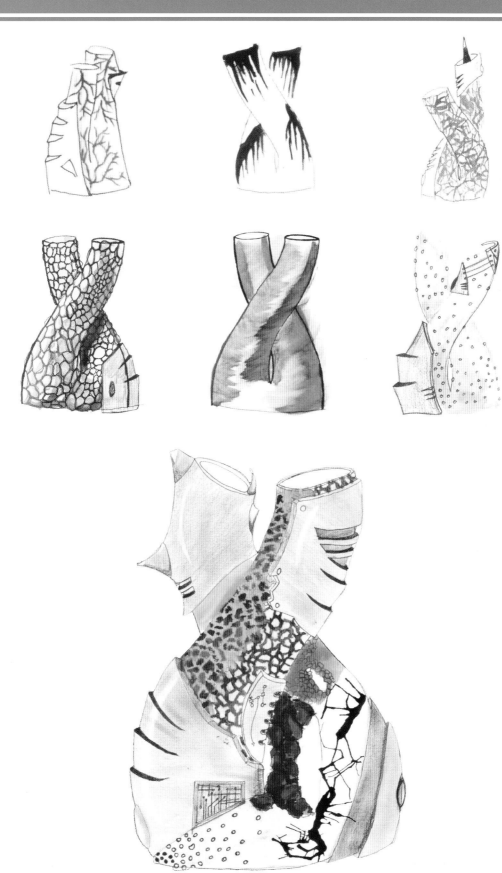

1.10 *Variations on a theme: developments of Josh's twisted blood vessels idea*

In developing his idea of the twisted blood vessels, Josh made many changes to the form, surfaces and colours, and at one stage he was keen to incorporate the idea of representing the mechanical replacement body parts used in modern medicine, though this was eventually rejected. By developing his ideas through a purposeful investigation, he developed his understanding of his source material and established the direction of his work.

Alternative approaches

Josh's work might have looked very different if his investigations into 'The Body' had led him to the work of Anthony Gormley or Elizabeth Frink.

Case study 4

Developing ideas in Fine Art

Josh's second project in his Unit 1 Portfolio of Work was based on the theme of 'Movement'. He had studied the work of the Futurists, Kandinsky and the contemporary artist Matt Brown from secondary sources to direct his own work towards abstraction (Figures 1.11, 1.13, and 1.14), and was particularly inspired by the athleticism of the sport known as 'Parkour'. He was confident enough in his drawing skills and in his knowledge of human anatomy to base his studies on the figure spinning, flying and falling through space. He became interested in how dancers move with poise and grace, and produced drawings in response (Figure 1.12). He also introduced ribbons and colour as additional **pictorial elements**, which gave his **compositions** greater fluency and movement.

As the work progressed, Josh developed the colour, content and composition of his drawings, before he finally chose to develop the figure of a sky diver.

Key terms

Pictorial elements: the component parts of a composition. For example trees, fields, buildings and sky are the pictorial elements of a rural landscape.

Composition: the arrangement of lines, shapes, forms and spaces in relation to each other.

Remember

By showing how your ideas have developed, you will be demonstrating important aspects of your 'creative journey'.

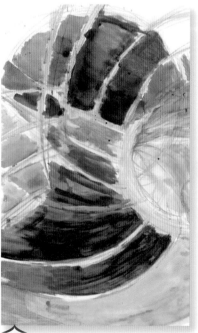

1.11 *Abstract movement*

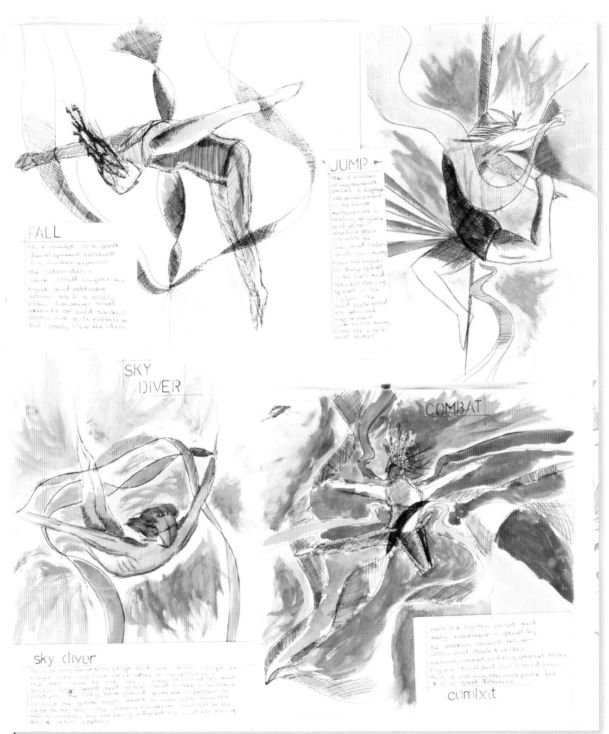

 1.12 *Annotated ideas sheet*

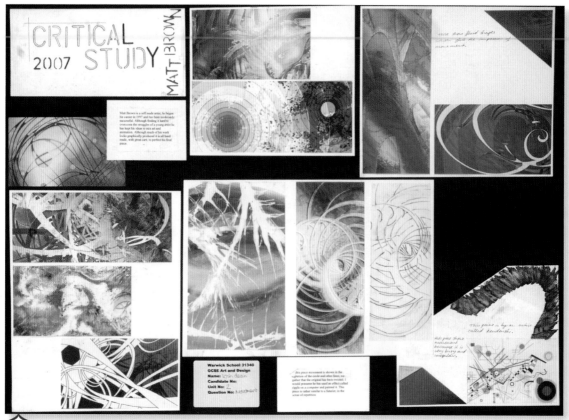

1.13 *Resource sheet with initial ideas*

1.14 *Wassily Kandinsky* Composition VIII *(1923)*

Establishing a focus to investigations

As you investigate a theme or topic, new thoughts, ideas and additional source material should feed into your work as it progresses. This will direct the flow of your work, sometimes prompting you to make changes in direction. Be open-minded and receptive to new ideas, even if they appear to change your original intentions, but take care to keep your investigation well focused. This is particularly important in Applied Art if you are working from a design brief where you have to meet the specific requirements of a client.

Do not be too eager to throw away studies you have made. It is important to show evidence of the alternatives you have investigated and the decisions and choices you have made as your work has progressed. In this way you can demonstrate and provide evidence of your thinking, and show the journey your work has taken in developing your ideas.

Through analysing your source material and making discoveries about its visual qualities and characteristics, you should establish a focus to your investigations and to the development of your idea. You might, for example, focus on light and colour, mood and atmosphere, texture and surface, form and volume, rhythm and movement, a narrative or story, an event or issue, a time or place, design and purpose, typography and image. Aim to develop a clear idea of what it is about your source material that is important to you. Through your work, ask questions about how it looks, what looks attractive, interesting, intriguing and exciting about it. What is it about your idea that you want to share with other people?

It is important to keep up the momentum of your work. Look back, and use what you have discovered to help you decide what to do next.

> **AQA   Examiner's tip**
>
> Your work may need to be seen as part of the moderation process. If any of the evidence of how ideas have developed in your work is stored in computer files, make sure they can be easily accessed for assessment by your teacher and the moderator by leaving clear written instructions.

> **AQA   Examiner's tip**
>
> If a lot of your development work takes place on a computer, make sure you save the stages of development either as **screen grabs** or prints.

> **Key terms**
>
> **Screen grab**: a way of saving images to show the stages of development in your work.

Case study 5

Working with a focus in the development of ideas in Fine Art

Having decided on sunsets as the focus of her investigation, and with Monet's paintings in mind, Lauren took photographs of sunsets on location. She explored her source material and investigated Monet's methods of working, analysing his composition, colour combinations and techniques. She found a connection to the development of her own ideas in Monet's fascination with lighting effects, the changes of light that occur throughout the day and how they alter mood and atmosphere. She also analysed Monet's handling of paint, and produced a series of studies in which she treated elements of her own compositions in different techniques (Figures 1.15 and 1.16). Lauren's study of Monet's work helped her to establish the focus to her investigations and informed the development of her ideas.

1.15 *Some of Lauren's additional source material and resulting studies*

⬭links

See Chapter 2 for ideas about experimenting with media, materials, processes and techniques.

See Chapter 3 for ideas about recording ideas, observations and insights.

1.16 *Decisions about how to develop ideas were based on these studies*

Approaches to the development of ideas

You might begin developing ideas from your investigation and analysis of your source material through, for example, drawing, painting, collage, a series of photographs or sequences of moving images from different locations. You might begin by analysing contextual material or other sources, or by experimenting with media, materials, processes and techniques. These activities will form an integral part of the process of your investigation and the development of your ideas.

You will arrange **pictorial** elements into a composition, or design elements into a design. All arrangements of the pictorial elements are compositions whether they are **figurative** or **abstract**. By changing the viewpoint, by moving material closer or further away, or by altering scale, you can dramatically improve its visual impact and the way in which it communicates the idea.

A key part of the process of developing ideas is the production of a working drawing, **plan**, **maquette**, model or prototype. This will focus your thoughts and investigations and alert you to possible problems in the composition or design of your work.

Key terms

Pictorial: the representation of space and depth. The illusion of three-dimensions in landscape painting or photography, for example.

Figurative: recognisable representations of the human figure, animals, objects and places.

Abstract: art that slightly, partially or completely departs from representing reality.

Plan: a drawing or diagram showing layout, arrangement or structure of something.

Maquette: a small 3D study or model, usually to scale, that explores shape, form and space, often translated from drawings. A maquette is like a 3D working drawing.

An artist developing ideas in Textile Design

Amy Houghton is a professional artist based in south-west England. After taking a degree in Mixed Media Textiles at Loughborough University she gained an MA in Textiles at Goldsmiths University of London. Her work brings her into contact with people of all ages. She has worked with children aged three to six, researching learning through creativity, has ran a young person's digital archive project, and created work inspired by older people's memories.

1.17 *Amy Houghton, cardigan study*

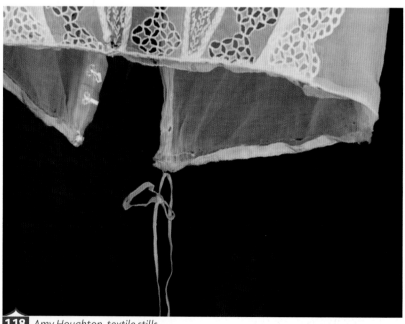

1.18 *Amy Houghton, textile stills*

1.19 *Amy Houghton, Cobbler, still from video, 2008*

Amy's current working practice involves using animation, video, installation and porcelain (see Figures 1.17–1.20). Her ideas come from exploring how we use antique textiles and old photographs to stimulate memories and nostalgia. She uses objects gathered from charity shops, junk shops, markets and eBay, which she unpicks and dismantles with forensic precision, trying to discover how the objects were constructed and used. She invents narratives about the objects and old photographs she collects from archives, their owners and the events they have been through. The use of new media places firmly in the present the historic objects that Amy uses in her practice.

1.20 *Amy Houghton, still from* White Shoes *video, 2008*

- In Fine Art you could investigate repeating, distorting, overlapping, cropping or combining images.
- In Graphic Communication you could investigate ways in which you might bring together images and **typography**, or visualise how packaging might be seen in multiples.
- In Textile Design you could produce samplers using unconventional materials, or 'draw' with stitching or bleach.
- In Sculpture and Three-Dimensional Design, drawings and maquettes can help understanding of volume and mass, and help visualise form and space.
- In Photography, contact prints and screen grabs of images can help to develop ideas.

Using digital media to develop ideas

Digital media can be a useful research tool for gathering information and images, but they can also provide opportunities to manipulate, combine and layer imagery, which can support investigations and the development of ideas. A range of digital media and techniques might be appropriate in the development of your work:

- scanning and printing images
- digital photography
- using computer software to generate and manipulate images
- using computer software to develop ideas about colour combinations or textures
- using film, video or sound to develop ideas
- using software to develop compositions, designs and layouts.

If you decide to develop your ideas using a computer, it is important to show evidence of the decisions you make so that the development

∞ links

See Chapter 2 for ways of refining ideas using resources, media and materials.

Remember

A key element in developing ideas is producing compositions, designs, maquettes, models, samples or contact sheets.

Key terms

Typography: the design of typefaces, and the layout of type.

of your ideas can be easily read and understood. Organising, saving and printing your work to show its development will demonstrate the progress in your work and the changes that have taken place.

In Case study 1, Lauren used a digital camera to produce the high-contrast silhouette images which formed the basis of the development of her ideas on landscapes and sunsets. Josh, in Case study 3, did much of his initial investigation using the internet, carefully selecting sources of information to inform the development of his ideas using twisted blood vessels. In Case study 4, he documented his three-dimensional work as it progressed, providing evidence of trial and error, and of experiments in scale and media. Nicole, in Case study 7, scanned her collages into a computer so that she could change the texture and colour of her designs, and experiment with the impact that different **typefaces** had on her imagery.

Remember

Save or print all the stages of the development of your ideas.

AQA Examiner's tip

It is much safer to always save work to the hard drive. Use your USB stick to transport documents between computers but do not use it in place of the hard drive.

Case study 7

Developing ideas using digital media in Applied Art

Nicole is responding to a brief provided by a local design group as part of her Applied course. The project involved making a presentation of her ideas to the company, in their studio, for a CD cover and insert with a nautical theme.

Nicole started by producing a '**mind map**' of ideas and possibilities. She decided that she would concentrate her investigations on four aspects of the theme: the sea, time, the stars and navigation.

Nicole decided that a technique combining **collage** with other media expressed her ideas in the most effective way. She produced several variations on her theme, scanning original artwork into a computer and manipulating each one by altering the colours and the contrast, and by adding imagery (Figures 1.22 and 1.23).

Key terms

Typeface: different styles of type. Also referred to as 'fonts', especially in connection with computers.

Mind map: a method of exploring thoughts and insights, and generating possible ideas quickly, often in written form – sometimes known as 'word storming', or a 'spider diagram'.

Collage: a technique for creating images by pasting together fragments of 2D and 3D materials.

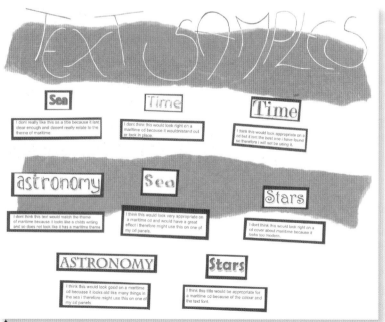

1.21 *Analysis of fonts*

did these alternatives so could see what colours and layout I wanted. Also I did some of them to go on different panels of my cd design but I later changed my mind and created better ones to replace them.

Three of the alternative designs I did by creating a collage and scanned then onto the computer and changed the colour, contrast and other things. I also added different images and bands of colour.

The one that wasn't made with a collage I got four different images for different themes of the project and did separate boxes for each image and wrote the theme above the image.

Navigation

Sta

Seafaring

Time

1.22 *Cover design ideas before the text was added*

Additional research material from websites helped Nicole select the most suitable typefaces for her four themes, (Figure 1.21). Layering the words and images digitally meant that she could control the size and position of the visual elements and make subtle adjustments to the layout.

1.23 *Refining the final idea: layering text and image*

Did you know ??????

It is good practice to back up your computer files in case the originals become lost or corrupted.

Alternative approaches

Another student, responding to the nautical theme in Case study 7, might have investigated sea shells or endangered marine species.

Using contextual materials and other sources to inform investigations

Contextual materials include works by other artists, craftspersons and designers. They can be examples such as:

- drawing, painting, printmaking, sculpture, land-art, installation, photography, film
- illustration, packaging design, designs for print, posters and promotional material
- textile design, fashion and costume, printed or dyed fabrics, constructed, stitched or embellished fabrics
- ceramics, constructions, installations, jewellery, product, interior, exhibition, theatre, architectural and environmental design
- photography, film, video.

Other sources of contextual material include architecture and architectural features, objects and artefacts that have a cultural significance from different places and times. These might be religious, ritual or symbolic objects that are connected with people's belief systems. They could be objects with a domestic, craft-based or industrial purpose, and may be functional, ornamental or decorative in nature.

Investigating contextual material and other sources should be integrated within your investigations and the development of your ideas, and should inform the progress of your work. This part of your investigation does not have to be something that takes place only at a particular stage of a project. The sources that you select should be relevant and appropriate, and not necessarily restricted to your **area of study**. For example, a Textile Design student could find inspiration from within the field of Graphic Communication, using sweet wrappers or packaging to develop their ideas.

Research into contextual sources should help to direct your investigations into your source material and ideas, and could help you to establish a clear sense of direction in your work. Contextual material can help you to look at and think about ideas and sources in different ways. For example, relevant sources for a project on Impressionist landscapes might include a selection of images by Monet, Seurat and Pissarro. By analysing the images and studying these artists' techniques you might see the potential in the pointillist technique used by Seurat and how it could inform your ideas. This in turn might trigger a search for additional material which might include investigating the dot screens used in the half-tone printing process or Aboriginal dot paintings or the work of Roy Lichtenstein. In Case study 9, Lauren realised that she needed to take more photographs of sunsets after investigating Monet's landscapes and analysing his painting techniques. Another student looking at the same theme with the same initial source material might become interested in the mood created in Monet's work and go on to investigate different ways of creating atmosphere in the work of other artists and photographers.

To inform your investigations, you might explore aspects such as:

- the time, place and circumstances in which works were produced
- how a subject or theme, idea or issue has been interpreted by others
- the ways in which techniques and materials have been used
- the use of **formal elements**
- how colour can create mood and atmosphere
- **format**, composition and **layout**
- texts, poetry, film or music
- materials which have a cultural, religious, ritual or symbolic meaning.

Key terms

Area of study: painting, sculpture, printed textiles, ceramics, illustration, packaging design, film, for instance.

Formal elements: the building blocks of art and design – line, shape, tone, texture, colour and form. These are often referred to as 'visual elements'.

Format: the type of layout and presentation of an image or design work, for example, whether it is 'portrait' or 'landscape', or how it is folded.

Layout: for example, the arrangement of images on a mount or study sheet, the arrangement of images and typography on a page.

AQA Examiner's tip

Make sure that your source materials are relevant to your ideas and be aware of their cultural significance.

Remember

- Contextual materials can be gathered throughout the development of a project.
- You can use contextual materials from any period, tradition or culture.
- You can look at any area of study to find contextual materials.

An artist using contextual materials in Textile Design

For her video installation called *Mary Croom's Dress*, artist Amy Houghton used stop-frame animation with soundtrack to show the forensic unpicking of a child's dress back-projected onto a frosted glass lightbox (Figures 1.24 and 1.25). The audio text that accompanies the piece tells of the unpicking and its relationship with the young Mary Croom in the photograph.

Amy explains how her contextual materials informed her ideas. 'I was given a child's Victorian dress by a magazine editor and three years later I came across an image of a virtually identical dress in a photograph. The dress was adorning a two-year-old Mary Croom, sitting there, clean, poised, neatly ironed and arranged; not the yellowed, worn and mended version that now lies in fragments on my desk. I want my Victorian dress to breathe so it can speak to me and show me the live video footage of its past but instead it whispers too quietly for me to hear. I'm like the child that is so eager to discover how the spider works that I have carefully pulled off its legs. I have taken the dress apart to discover more about how it is made. Under the penetrating light I can see its skeleton, I now understand its stitch structure and I discover the order in which it was pieced together.'

Amy explored a number of alternatives before deciding that it worked best in close-up. She tried manipulating the images, using Adobe Photoshop to invert the colours so that it would look more like an X-ray. She also tried many different ways to show the video animation: projecting it on a wall, projecting it onto layers of glass, showing it on a television and computer monitor. In the end, she back-projected it onto frosted glass placed in a frame on a wall, so that it looked like a scientific lightbox.

She lists various artists' works as influences, including those by Rachel Whiteread, Cornelia Parker, Christo and Grayson Perry, in addition to the cast figures of Pompeii and a number of books and films.

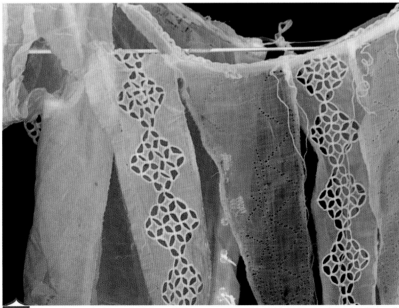

1.24 Mary Croom's dress, *2006, a still from an animation which shows the unpicking of a child's Victorian dress*

1.25 Mary Croom's dress, *2006, video installation*

Case study 9

Using contextual material in Fine Art

Lauren's interest in Impressionist landscapes was prompted by her fascination with the effects of light on water, and she took a number of photographs featuring sunsets and strong lighting effects. In her initial contextual studies she investigated the work of five impressionist artists, Cassatt, Monet, Sisley, Pissarro and Seurat, and she made studies of well-known works by each of them. This gave her insights into the compositions and techniques, and a greater understanding of the cultural context in which the works were produced. Two of the artists seemed to offer the best links to her own ideas, and she chose to investigate Monet and Seurat in more depth.

She analysed the scientific and meticulous approach to colour adopted by Seurat, through her own studies and media experiments, but she realised that the ideas behind Monet's work, the vague shapes and blurred edges, the depiction of motion and change, was to have the strongest influence on the development of her own ideas, (Figures 1.26 to 1.28). As she says on one of her

1.26 *Investigating the work of Claude Monet*

1.27 *Claude Monet,* Impression: Sunrise *(1874)*

preparation sheets, 'Monet wanted to create a sense of motion and change as well as capturing light. He used big, broken brush strokes to apply the colour. These are visible when viewed closely and help to create a sense of direction by manipulating the size, shape and angle. Rather than create the colours on a palette, most of the mixing was done on the canvas. I particularly like the water scenes. Unlike Seurat's work I find Monet's more emotive due to the lack of scientific theory. He fills the page with colours rather than unnecessary objects which complicate the piece.'

With the knowledge and understanding that came from the study of her contextual material, Lauren was able to develop her own ideas with purpose and confidence.

1.28 *Analysing Monet's technique*

Using contextual material in Applied Art

Nicole wanted to include lots of fragments of visual information overlaid with text in a busy composition, so she decided to produce images using collage for her CD sleeve design. During her investigations into suitable contextual materials she discovered the work of Robert Rauschenberg (Figure 1.29), whose work has a style and method similar to those expressed in her own ideas. She liked the compositions of overlapping slabs of bright colours, and the painterly qualities in Rauschenberg's paintings that she saw during analysis of his work.

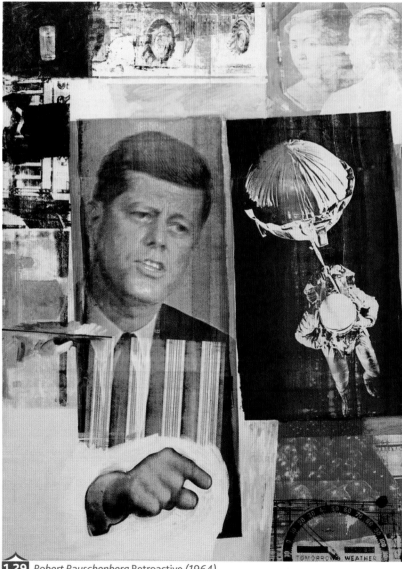

1.29 *Robert Rauschenberg* Retroactive (1964)

She produced a series of her own collages, informed by the work of Rauschenberg, using torn paper, coloured tissue and found images. By scanning them and using Adobe Photoshop she was able to manipulate her images by subtly changing their **colourways** while retaining the essence of her colourful originals. Nicole investigated suitable fonts and incorporated text into her designs.

Key terms

Colourway: a range of colour combinations for a design, layout, fabric or pattern.

1.30 *Nicole's CD sleeve designs*

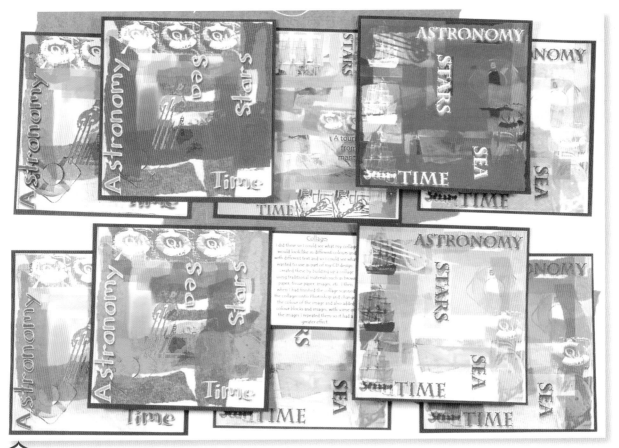

1.31 *Scanned collages combining images and text*

What is appropriate contextual material?

Contextual materials can be selected from a wide range of sources. They can take many forms (see Figures 1.32–1.34) and be used in various ways to inform your investigations and the development of your ideas. You might select material because it has a similar subject and content to your own work. A range of contextual material might show different or contrasting ways of responding to an idea. It might help you to consider and to reflect on other ways of directing and developing your work. You might use contextual material to inform your handling of a particular medium or technique, to explore colour combinations or tonal relationships.

1.32 *Eadweard Muybridge* Animal Locomotion *(1887)*

It is important that the contextual materials you select are appropriate to your intentions. If, for example, you are studying Fine Art, you might select material which is entirely drawing and painting but you might also explore relevant material from other areas of art and design.

Here are some examples:

- Work on the theme of 'The Body' in Fine Art might lead to an investigation of the photography of Eadweard Muybridge, medical textbooks, or the paintings of Francis Bacon or Lucian Freud.

- In Graphic Communication, a packaging project might include a study of paper engineering, the work of architect, designer and inventor Buckminster Fuller, or the colour theories of Johannes Itten, as well as examples of packaging designers' work.

- In Textile Design, the theme of 'Identity' might result in researching military uniforms and insignia, scientific images of fingerprints, the structure of deoxyribonucleic acid (DNA), as well as examples of constructed textiles.

- In Three-Dimensional Design, a study of a natural object might lead to an investigation into Art Nouveau furniture, poster and tableware designs, as well as examples of ceramics.

- In Photography, a study based on 'Buildings' might involve looking at the work of artists such as Lyonel Feininger as well as photographers.

1.33 *Émile Gallé Art Nouveau cabinet (c1890)*

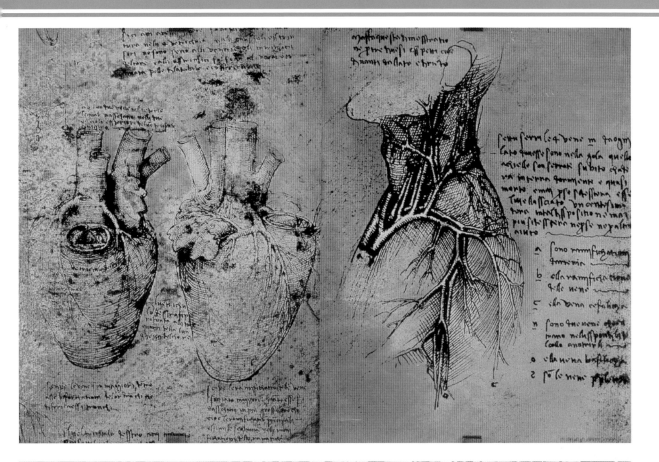

1.34 *Relevant contextual materials can be gathered from a wide variety of sources: from anatomical drawings by Leonardo da Vinci (top) to medals (including the Victoria Cross) awarded for bravery at Arnhem, Netherlands during the Second World War*

Finding suitable contextual material in Fine Art

During his investigation on the theme of 'Movement', Josh found a diverse range of contextual material by looking for suitable visual references both within and beyond his area of study. He began by looking at the work of the Futurists (Figure 1.37), and Wassily Kandinsky, whose work he liked for its 'busy and irregular' qualities but this was rejected due to its angularity. Instead, on the internet he discovered the work of contemporary artist Matt Brown, which was to have the strongest influence on the development of his own ideas. The twisted, abstract forms in Brown's work suggested movement and light to him, and the idea of introducing ribbons into his compositions came directly from the swirling shapes in Brown's paintings (Figure 1.35). He was also inspired by

Remember

- Source material can be collected throughout the investigation and development of your work.
- Contemporary artists and designers can be as relevant to your investigations as those from the past.

1.35 *Matt Brown* A Play on Light no. 129

1.36 *Study sheet: moving figures*

Parkour (also known as 'PK' or 'Free Running') and he found photographs of figures running, jumping and spinning through space, silhouetted against the sky (Figure 1.36). These images informed Josh's own figure drawings.

∞links

For more examples of Matt Brown's work, go to **www.mattbrownart.com**

1.37 *Giacomo Balla* Lines of Movement and Dynamic Succession *(1913)*

Locating contextual materials

The most obvious places to find suitable contextual materials such as books, magazines, periodicals, catalogues and DVDs, are the libraries in your art department and school or college, and in your local library. Many towns also have galleries and museums where you can experience works of art, objects and artefacts at first hand. However, you may want to see work of a more specific nature. There are galleries and museums dedicated to design, photography, packaging, cartoons, fashion and textiles to visit in person or online, and many artists and designers have their own websites. The internet is a powerful research tool, allowing you to view objects and images that might be unavailable by other means, and it can often throw up unexpected results when you are looking to widen your investigation. Remember that with so much information available, you should be selective and keep the focus of your investigation.

> **Remember**
>
> Don't collect contextual materials randomly or thoughtlessly.

> **Remember**
>
> Record relevant data on sources such as the artist's name, the title and date of the work, wherever possible.

Using contextual materials in Three-Dimensional Design

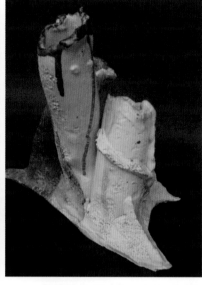

1.38 *Sculptures based on blood vessels*

∞ links

For more examples of
Kate Malone's ceramics, go to
www.kmaloneceramics.clara.net/

Josh's ideas in his Portfolio Project on 'The Body' were informed by the work of ceramicist Kate Malone. Josh was initially attracted to Malone's work by the way she had interpreted natural objects such as exotic plants and flowers. The bright colours, the use of pebble glazes and the bulbous forms were all influential in the development of Josh's own work based on blood vessels and veins. As he says, '...the arms like tentacles resemble the blood veins and arteries extending and engulfing the object. My ideas use the nerve patterns but I think these bloody patterns are very close to what I am trying to invent.'

1.39 *Kate Malone* Big Boy Gourd *(2002)*

Analysing contextual material

The purpose of analysing and exploring contextual materials is to help you to develop your understanding of how and why techniques and media have been used and how compositions, designs and layouts work, to inform your own investigations and the development of your ideas. Analysing contextual materials should also develop your understanding of different ways that artists and designers have responded to ideas and help you to understand the cultural significance of artefacts and works of art, craft and design.

You can analyse contextual material in various ways: by making analytical studies through drawing and painting, copying areas of images to discover the way a medium has been handled, looking at techniques such as the way charcoal has been used to create tonal values, light and dark, the way that paint has been built up in thick, impasto layers or in thin, transparent washes. You could analyse the ways in which colour combinations have been used to make subtleties or contrasts, or the way in which colour has been used to create an atmosphere, to make connections between areas of an image or to give emphasis. It might be appropriate for you to make studies that compare the ways that different artists have responded to the landscape or to the

1.40 *Compositional analysis*

1.41 *Georges Seurat* Sunday Afternoon on the Island of the Grande Jatte *(1884–86)*

kerboodle!

portrait, or the ways that textures have been created and used by a particular artist or designer.

You might explore composition by making drawings or diagrams that analyse the way that our eyes are led around an image from one shape or form to another, looking at eye level, viewpoint, the ways that lines and shapes connect together and create movement, the balance between positive and negative shapes, the ways that space and scale are used, or how parts of an image relate to each other.

It is not always possible to analyse in a purely practical way through drawings, diagrams and colour studies. For example, analysing the use of tone and texture in a series of photographs, the relationship between image and typography in a page layout, or the aesthetic and functional aspects of a product design might be more appropriate in the form of notes or annotated images.

▉ Developing analytical and cultural understanding

Analytical understanding can be demonstrated in your work in several ways. In selecting a starting point you will show evidence of your understanding in analysing what is suggested by the idea, theme or issue. If you are working to a design brief you will demonstrate understanding in analysing what is required by the brief or a client. Analytical understanding will also be evident in the ways that you develop your investigations and your ideas. You will analyse your source materials using skills, media and techniques that are appropriate to your area of study. You will show analytical understanding in the ways that your investigations and ideas progress, by analysing problems and in making informed decisions in the development of your ideas.

You can show evidence of analytical understanding in several ways:

▉ analysing and understanding ideas and starting points

▉ analysing and understanding your source materials

▉ making connections between one image and another

▉ showing how one image leads to developments in others

▉ indicating similarities between your work and that of other artists

▉ demonstrating your preferences for particular images, ideas, techniques, processes and media.

Analytical and cultural understanding can be demonstrated in the way that you select, analyse and respond to contextual materials and other sources that are appropriate to your investigations and the development of your ideas. Cultural understanding is about the ways that you demonstrate your understanding of the context of a work of art, craft or design. This includes an awareness and understanding of aspects such as:

▉ when and where a work was made; its time and place

▉ the ways that a work is part of and reflects its cultural background

▉ different ways of seeing the world visually

▉ a work's purpose and meaning

▉ a work's practical, symbolic, spiritual, religious or ritual function and significance.

⊂⊃ links

See Chapter 3 for ideas about recording your observations and insights.

Did you know ??????

You do not have to use artists from the past or famous artists. It is just as acceptable to choose contemporary artists, or ones that are not well known.

For example, Constructivist painting, graphics and architecture produced in Russia in the period which followed the Russian Revolution has a distinct character that reflects its time and its culture. The woodcuts by Hokusai, a 19th-century Japanese artist, reflect a way of seeing the natural world that is flat and decorative, unlike the paintings of John Constable which are romantic and pictorial. The Art Nouveau tableware and jewellery designs of Archibald Knox have a distinctively decorative character that is very different from the geometrical architecture, constructions and furniture designs of Gerrit Rietveld. In the same way, the art of Ancient Egypt has a character that is distinct from that of Native American cultures.

Using contextual material to inform the development of ideas

Contextual material can help to develop your focus and direction in analysing your source material and, sometimes, the contextual material itself might be the source or starting point for your ideas. You might, for example, base your ideas on the investigation of Chinese dragons or art of the Mayan culture.

Looking at the ways in which other artists or designers have responded to a particular theme or design problem can stimulate your own ideas and help you to think visually. It can suggest techniques, media and methods of working that you can incorporate into your work and it can give you guidance and support in looking for alternatives and in solving problems.

Contextual material can inform the development of your work in a number of ways. It can:

- provide a starting point for your own ideas
- provide alternative ways of looking at ideas
- inform your approach and response to source material
- provide insights into composition, design and layout
- provide insights into colour, tone and texture
- help you to resolve problems
- help you to develop analyical and cultural understanding.

Case study 12

An artist using contextual materials in Textile Design

The process of producing porcelain, a delicate, translucent material made from china clay found in the West Country near St Austell, fascinates the artist Amy Houghton. As well as reanimating objects using animation and video in her work, Amy creates 3D stills of textile objects by transforming them in porcelain. Through her explorations into the combination, integration and transformation of textiles, metals and porcelain, she has created a series of porcelain and macramé wire 'knitted landscapes' (Figures 1.42 and 1.43). These pieces ask questions about the meaning of objects and the time in which they exist, and the use of porcelain is a reminder of the impermanence of time.

1.42 Knitted landscape 2, *2005*

1.43 Knitted landscape 5, *2005*

1.44 *Broderie Anglaise Light*

∞links

See Chapter 3 for ways to record ideas.

Learning outcomes

Having read this chapter you should now be able to:

investigate an idea, theme or issue from a starting point or brief

develop an idea, issue or theme for which you can collect appropriate resources

select from alternative ideas and approaches as your work develops

use contextual and other sources to inform the development of your ideas

demonstrate analytical and cultural understanding in your investigations and in the development of your ideas.

There are many different ways of using resources, media, materials, techniques and processes to investigate sources, explore themes, develop ideas, and create and produce artistic responses. Different types of starting points can suggest particular features such as colour, texture, structure or form while others may direct your investigation to a specific range of materials or techniques such as paint, clay, textiles or animation. It is important that you consider ideas, sources, project briefs, contextual references or starting points to help you to direct your experiments with media and materials.

Identify the media and materials available to you. Develop your understanding of their properties and find out different ways you could use them. Remember that experimenting with new techniques can be daunting but try not to be discouraged and don't worry if your initial attempts seem less than satisfactory. Often several experiments may be required before you feel confident selecting and applying materials and techniques. Finding the effects you want may take several attempts but by building sufficient confidence in your technical skills you should be able to achieve the effects you require. As your understanding of a process improves, results can be reviewed and you can refine your ideas.

2.1 *Using digital manipulation*

Selecting and using appropriate resources and media

In your work, provide evidence that your resources and materials have been chosen and explored to help you further your ideas. This may be demonstrated by showing the investigation of themes in a variety of ways and by experimenting with different types of **media** throughout your course of study. This will help you to create a working vocabulary of resources, practical knowledge and technical skills.

So how do you start to select which materials to use to develop your thoughts and ideas? Sources can provide a diverse range of starting points and collected images, photographs, sketches and references to the work of others may suggest qualities which can be explored through a diversity of media and technique. Studies could evolve from an investigation of visual elements such as line, shape, pattern, colour or composition or be inspired by how an artist, designer or craftsperson has used a material.

For example an image from a photograph may be developed into a painting in acrylic in order to explore form or a greater depth of colour while references to the designs of an artist such as Matisse may encourage experiments in the manipulation of cut or torn paper. A wish to understand more about the properties of a particular product could also provide a positive source. The opportunity to participate in a pottery workshop may inspire use of the skills learned and allow for the creative development of 3D work through the confident handling of clay.

It is important to first establish which characteristics of your chosen source material you wish to investigate. You can then select an appropriate variety of resources and materials to help you explore them.

In Case study 14 below, for example, numerous photographs, test studies and samples illustrate:

- a growing confidence in identifying resources
- choosing suitable materials to interpret key features
- practise in using techniques.

Key terms

Media: the materials used to create a piece of art work such as pencil, paint, oil pastel, charcoal, chalk, pen and ink, fabric, clay.

links

See Chapter 1 for more examples of the work of Matisse.

Case study 14

Selecting resources and materials to develop ideas in Fine Art

Lauren has produced a portfolio that includes a sketchbook of media experiments based on three different starting points. A brief set by her teacher led to an A1 sheet with a finished painting for one theme. A project based on natural forms allowed her to explore the characteristics of acrylic painting and learn how to create a drypoint print. A folder of photographic resources and **frottage** sheets encouraged references and analysis of how Greg Fuller and Antoni Tápies selected and employed materials; these inspired seven A1 study boards and two A1 outcome sheets themed 'Surfaces'.

Traditional materials including pencils, acrylic paint and paper collage were chosen to investigate the abstract shapes and patterns suggested by an observational study of collected objects. Lauren found the qualities achieved by tearing and layering paper were effective. She experimented with tissue, shiny magazine pages and paper with text to assess the most appropriate way to show a harmony of colour, pattern and texture. She added oil pastel to the collage

Key terms

Frottage: the transfer of a relief image or surface by placing a sheet of paper over the design and rubbing it firmly with crayon, chalk or charcoal.

2.2 *Sketchbook sheets showing paper experiments*

to increase the tactile appearance and this led to brushing a **wash** of paint over the ripped paper (Figure.2.2). In a later assignment on natural forms, Lauren's pencil drawings and handling of colour had become more assured and evolved into experiments with drypoint etching and an acrylic painting. In a third project, her personal photographs of bricks, wood, rust and frottage suggested tactile qualities of uneven surfaces. Lauren's knowledge of using creative materials developed and she chose sand, **bitumen**, pva glue, **gesso** and varnish to explore the differences between rough and smooth surfaces (Figure 2.3).

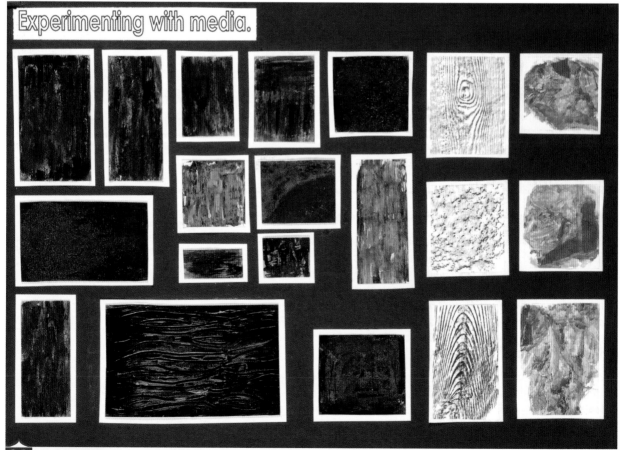

Experimenting with media.

2.3 *Study sheet; experimenting with media*

Using the marks provided by the frottage to suggest the shapes, forms and textures for her experiments with mixed media, Lauren layered sand, glue, bitumen and paint and tried scraping the media in different directions to imply the grain of wood. By adding ink and sand between layers of varnish she was able to represent the streaked appearance of rust.

The use of Adobe Photoshop (Figure 2.4), enabled Lauren to adjust her digital photographs and enhance line, colour, tone and the illusion of texture. She used the 'burn' and 'dodge' tools to add lights and darks; and by moving the zoom she could control the areas she wished to focus on, and exaggerate areas of tone. Two outcomes were produced. One showed her handling of mixed media and a second demonstrated her knowledge of photographic manipulation (Figure 2.1).

In each set of work Lauren chose materials that would help her investigate her sources in a personal manner. She learned new skills to broaden her technical range and considered which materials would be most appropriate in helping her realise her intentions. In her investigation of surfaces the media she used enabled her to create her own tactile surfaces. By rubbing sand onto paint and mixing glue, gesso, inks and varnish within her compositions she was able to demonstrate a clear link between her ideas on texture and the materials needed to develop her creative ability in expressing them.

AQA Examiner's tip

When referring to a work by an artist, designer or craftsperson make sure you show an understanding of why you find it relevant to the development of your ideas; think about the materials that were used and how they were applied.

Did you know ??????

The Catalan painter Tàpies applied thick impasto to canvas, added marble dust to paint and scratched into the surface of his paintings. He often used unconventional materials such as waste paper, string, rags and even bits of furniture in paintings.

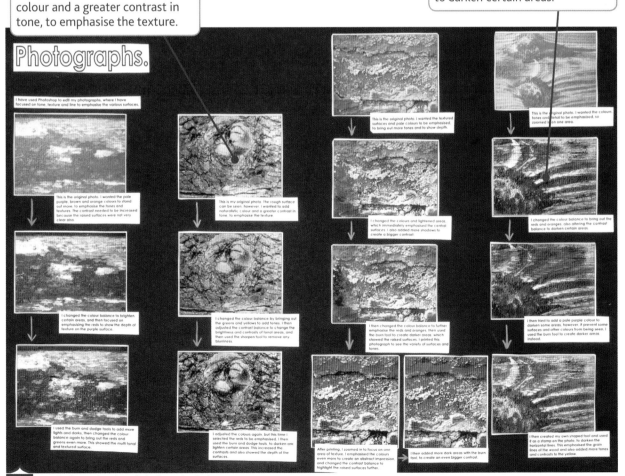

2.4   *Study sheet showing digital manipulation*

Finding appropriate media

In Case study 14, Lauren's sketchbook and study boards demonstrate the success and importance of selecting the appropriate media to translate images and thoughts. Not all Lauren's samples were successful but she used her discoveries to help evaluate her experiments and to plan how to push her technical range forward. As she became more adventurous in handling materials her work became more personal and imaginative. She discovered that a material can be exploited to express more than one quality and by manipulating features such as the consistency or transparency of paint, size and type of brush, bleed of ink or grade of paper, subtle contrasts could be introduced.

Finding the media most suited to interpreting your source material and developing your intentions is best achieved by trying out different processes, analysing your results and trying further experiments. Some of the products, materials and processes you may like to consider are:

- pencils in different grades such as B, 2B, 4B, 6B, HB, H
- biro, fine liner, pen and ink
- charcoal, graphite sticks, white and coloured chalks
- **drypoint etching**
- water-soluble pencils and crayons
- oil pastels, oil bars and paint sticks
- acrylic, watercolour, **gouache** and oil paint
- lino cuts
- cut paper or blocked stencils
- collage using items such as paper, card, material, metal, found and recycled objects
- frottage, **collagraph**
- **batik**, starch or resist media
- photography, digital imagery, animation and image manipulation
- assorted grades of paper such as watercolour, tissue, bubble-wrap, newsprint, brown or corrugated
- clay, plaster, Mod-Roc and resin
- wire, willow withe
- fabric, thread, net and felt.

Kate Fenton (see Case study 29 in Chapter 3) found that by selecting and practising with pencil, fine pen, ink, paint and pastel, she could record the shape, structure and linear form of shells. She used the same process several times and tried different coloured pastel overlays for scratching out drawings. Grey, white and cream paper provided alternative grounds for black ink and white line studies (Figure 2.5).

∞ links

Lauren was inspired by materials and techniques used by Greg Fuller and Antoni Tápies. For more ideas on using contextual sources to help develop ideas see Chapter 1.

∞ links

For more examples of the materials Kate used see Chapter 3.

Key terms

Drypoint printing: the production of a print by scratching an image into an acrylic or soft metal plate with a sharp tool. The plate is then inked and printed.

Gouache: an opaque paint which can be mixed with water and applied to a surface to give a flat, smooth and dense colour.

Collagraph: a print produced by inking an image block created from pieced cardboard, paper, string, etc.

Batik: the application of hot wax to a surface prior to colouring with dye. Successive additions of wax and dye can be built up to create a richly coloured piece.

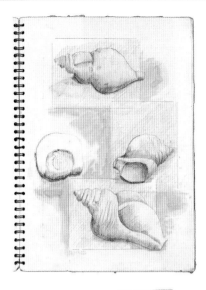

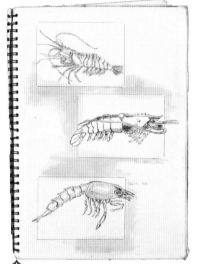
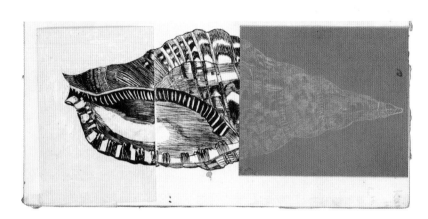

2.5 *Sketchbook pages demonstrating the use of different media to record observations*

Case study 15

Choosing materials and processes to develop ideas in Art and Design

The theme of 'Identity' for an Externally Set Task enabled Jennifer to choose materials she had experience of using and practice in applying during her course of study. She completed an A3 sketchbook during the preparatory period which included collected pictures, personal photographs, pencil drawings on coloured chalk grounds, painted portraits and found materials applied to both distressed and raised-surface collaged paper. Pencil sketches of sculptures by Andy Goldsworthy, Henry Moore and Barbara Hepworth helped her understand the different structures which could be used to represent a sense of a figurative form. During the timed 10-hour session she produced a mixed media A1 study and a memory box mounted on a textured background (Figure 2.6).

▶

2.6 *Mixed media outcomes*

The sketchbook demonstrates Jennifer's knowledge of how to identify and select appropriate materials and processes. She began by finding photographs which recorded different stages of her life: pictures of when she was a baby, with her siblings, friends and family. She then wrote down song lyrics and bits of text that have shaped her moods or influenced her feelings. Next she thought about how artists have depicted the figurative form and developed powerful portraits where the application and colour of the paint helped to present a sense of character.

The base material that marks and images are applied to is important in this project. By creating pages which visually help to extend and project ideas Jennifer has used her choice of media to push her project forward. Her notes refer to colour as well as a sense of being and this is used to direct the tones of acrylic, chalk and pastel that are brushed, rubbed and scrubbed onto paper. For some studies, cut and torn cardboard, tissue and newspaper have been built up on the page, covered with a ground and then worked into with bold, rapid brushstrokes of thick paint. Scorched card overworked with wax and paint reflects a sense of energy. Towards the end of her research Jennifer considered the materials she needed to complete her final outcomes. She listed the articles to be fitted into her box and noted qualities she wanted to suggest such as smell and taste; her list included buttons, feathers, personal objects, mirrors, text and photographs.

In the supervised period of 10 hours Jennifer demonstrated that she could successfully use her chosen materials. The time she had spent experimenting with building up an appropriate surface, thinking about which media could accommodate strong colour and underlying text, was time well spent. Her final mixed media panel depicts a larger size of lettering than she originally considered, and allows her to demonstrate fluid painting rather than tight pen work, and so is more appropriate for the dramatic composition. The selection of paint and brush ensures an effective result. In her memory box, materials are still used with impact but there is a greater sense of control. In this piece, text in a lighter pen fades into the background and this too allows for greater focus on the articles placed in the box. The application of paint and tissue has contributed to the outcome.

> **AQA Examiner's tip**
>
> Always use the preparation period to experiment with the materials and processes you intend to use in an Externally Set Task.
>
> Work out a time plan and make sure you have all the materials and equipment that you need.

> **Did you know ??????**
>
> Another artist well-known for creating art within the structure of a box was Joseph Cornell. He placed everyday objects, found items, fragments of once treasured possessions and photographs into glass-fronted boxes to suggest a surreal world.

Experimenting with materials, techniques and processes

The Specification requires you to select and explore materials that are appropriate to your intentions and course of study. This encourages you to:

- investigate techniques you may not be familiar with
- learn new working methods
- experiment with resources
- develop your skills in handling media, processes and techniques
- increase your confidence
- extend your visual vocabulary.

In both case studies in this chapter students needed to develop their knowledge and handling of media by exploring methods of application, characteristics of materials, and influences of colour, texture, line and scale. Lauren needed to find out exactly how much glue she must add to the sand to make it stick and how viscous her paint and bitumen mix needed to be before she could successfully scratch into it. Jennifer had to work out the time required for her textured board to dry before she could successfully write on top of it with a biro. As they manipulated wet tissue, mixed paint and etched into surfaces both students gained a valuable understanding of their materials and the opportunities specific properties suggested. They recorded their experiments and findings through sketchbook studies, annotations and sample boards.

Using materials to explore linear quality

When selecting media it is also important to remember that different materials can be used to express different qualities. Sometimes the images you wish to show may be suited more to one medium than another. Equally, some qualities and characteristics of your source material might be expressed in more than one medium. Lauren discovered that the linear quality of her pencil drawings could be sustained and extended into drypoint as a similar style of mark-making was required. She initially used a black fine line pen to represent the etching tool and used this to gain an impression of how **cross-hatching**, hard, bold lines and blocked-in sections could work. Once she felt confident in her composition she learned how to scratch the plate, apply and remove ink and create a print (Figure 2.7).

Key terms

Cross-hatching: shading by intersecting parallel lines.

Over-painting: applying repeated layers of paint to a surface. The paint can be allowed to dry before each layer is applied or subsequent layers may be built up in different paint consistencies or with different brush sizes to create a sense of texture.

2.7 *A pencil sketch evolves into a drypoint print*

Exploring a theme using paint

Lauren (Case study 5, Chapter 1) analysed how the Impressionists applied paint to a canvas. She looked at the texture of the surface and considered whether paint had been put down in thin layers, whether it was built up and over-painted, or applied rapidly. This led her to explore the potential of acrylic. In her studies of skies, Lauren considered how the nature of brushstrokes could help her respond to her sources. Through six landscape compositions she varied the painting technique between short brushstrokes which dabbed colour across the surface, and long horizontal marks which dragged the paint to produce a subtle blending of tones. **Over-painting** created a heavy surface for the sky and by putting an excessive amount of paint on her brush Lauren extended the **illusion** of **weight** between land and sky (Figure 2.8).

⚭ **links**

See Chapter 1 for more evidence of Lauren's painting skills. See Case study 44 in Chapter 4 for examples of how Katherine used brushstrokes to suggest the weight and direction of folds in fabric.

Key terms

Illusion: the creation of a deceptive appearance. For example, the illusion of a 3-D object drawn on a flat sheet of paper.

Weight: creating the impression that something is heavy.

More painting experiments

Use watercolour paint to achieve a translucent or transparent effect; build up layers of washes.

Use water to thin paint and try bleeding colours together.

Use gouache for more opaque colour, particularly if you want to achieve a flat surface.

Exploring a theme using 3D materials

If you are working with 3D materials it is also important that you experiment with your medium to discover the possibilities it can offer. For example in Case study 38 (Chapter 4) Jake experiments in using clay. He presses a variety of different textured articles into the clay in order to investigate the surfaces they create. As his experiments become more inventive he explores how he can extend his ideas by cutting and joining clay pieces together, trailing slips and adding glazes.

If you decide to use plaster, wire, metal or fabric it is important that you investigate and experiment with the properties of the material and then try different ways of exploiting its characteristics. Tester samples, small maquettes and sculptures can all help you to record your findings.

2.8 *Painting experiments illustrate diversity in brushstroke*

Case study 16

An artist selecting resources and materials to develop ideas in Three-Dimensional Design

Sarah McCormack trained for a BA (Hons) in 3D design and specialised in stained glass and ceramics when she was at college. Now Sarah finds clay the most suitable material for the translation of her ideas. Since leaving art college she has worked with school groups and on community projects to create ceramic pieces. She has a studio in Plymouth where she currently produces pottery. Her current work involves creating ceramic clocks inspired by memories of her childhood and views from the window of her studio (Figure 2.9). She can see the sea from her workspace. Images of waves, boats and birds such as seagulls and pigeons, as well as the Victorian roof tiles of nearby houses often provide ideas which she explores through the medium of clay.

Sarah combines slab and coiling techniques as these enable her to manipulate the material into the most appropriate 3D shapes and forms. She experiments with red earthenware, buff mid-temperature and white earthenware and

2.9 *Sarah McCormack at work in her studio*

2.10 *Slab-built pieces in red and buff clay*

2.11 Clay samples based on natural forms

2.12 Clay stamps are created to help reproduce an image

2.13 Sarah's grandmother's clock inspired her ideas for shape and structure

finds that specific types of clay enable her to create different surface qualities (Figure 2.10). Texture and image are important and in previous projects Sarah has used hand-carved stamps to imprint motifs into ceramic paintings. She has now adapted this process to help her to make her clay clocks. The shapes of tiny fish, ammonites, boats and leaves are sketched and a maquette is made from rolled clay. A pattern is then produced from the most successful shapes so that the motif and scale can be repeated as accurately as possible (Figures 2.11 and 2.12).

Sarah's initial inspiration for clocks came from an image of her grandmother's clock. It was made of metal and is quite architectural in design, (Figure 2.13). Sarah made a number of drawings of this clock from different angles and modified her observations until she found a version that she thought she could translate into clay. The domed tops, however, proved a problem and Sarah knew from her understanding of how clay could be manipulated that a design similar to her sketches would be difficult to recreate. Her understanding of the properties of the material enabled her to experiment with a construction method which would allow her to achieve a successful form (Figure 2.14).

Before firing a design Sarah always experiments with glazes and makes numerous test pieces. She finds that as her designs evolve it is important to select the correct glaze. Experience has taught her that it is easy to ruin a good piece with a bad glaze.

2.14 *Clay clocks illustrate an understanding of how the material defines the construction method and shape*

Case study 10

Experimenting with materials and techniques in Textile Design

Isobelle used textile materials of both a 2D and 3D nature to respond to an Externally Set Task. She created a series of concertina study boards to demonstrate her preparatory studies (Figure 2.15), and in the period of supervised time completed a dyed and stitched decorative panel.

Isobelle explored creative machine embroidery, the application of dyes to cotton, cut work, couching yarns and the selection of appropriate threads, ribbons, net and fabrics during the development of her Portfolio studies. She used her knowledge to guide her experiments with materials and techniques in response to the suggested theme 'Shorelines'. Photographs and sketches of lobster pots, seaweed, rocks, pebbles, waves and the receding tide line helped her focus on the shapes, colours, patterns and textures observed along a familiar stretch of coastline. Once she had assembled her resources and had an idea of the visual elements she wished to explore she was able to further her intentions by experimenting with materials and techniques. She considered the shape of waves, the colour of the wet shoreline, the pattern on the tentacles of an octopus and the texture of seaweed.

> ### Remember
> ▤ Work safely with materials and equipment.
> ▤ Think of your own safety and that of others around you.

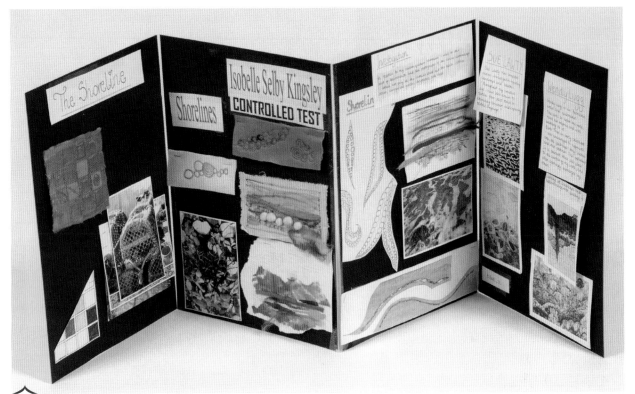

2.15 *Section of preparatory studies for Textile Design Externally Set Task*

Using research work to suggest textile materials and techniques

Isobelle's line drawings and torn paper collages suggested basic shapes and uneven bands of horizontal colour. She found that torn strips of fabric and textured yarns could be arranged to reflect a similar format. By twisting threads and stitching over the braids with a sewing machine Isobelle could hold the composition in place and the flow of the line could then be extended by adding free machine work as well as waves of straight and zig-zag stitches (Figure 2.16).

Images of pebbles and stones were amongst the most distinctive in Isobelle's research work and she wanted to recreate them in textiles. She experimented with using a machine attachment which allowed her to stitch in a circular motion. Isobelle lined different sizes of circles next to each other to give the illusion of a pebbly beach. By adding nets she was able to introduce subtle variations of tone. These 'pebbles' however were flat and Isobelle wanted a more 3D appearance. She tried rolling small pieces of wadding into a ball and

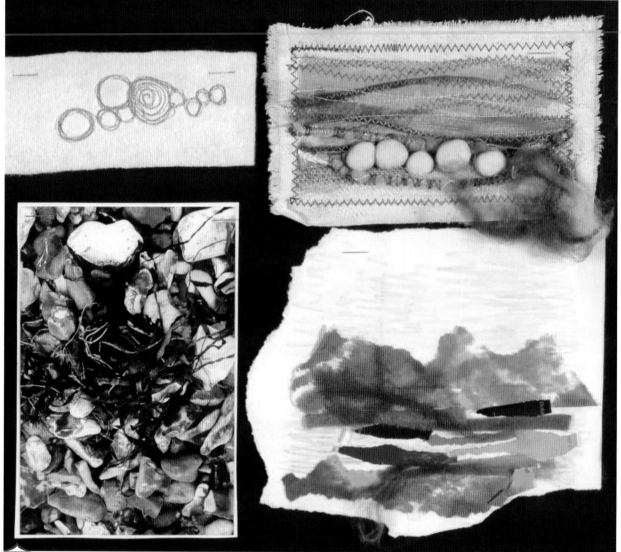

2.16 *Experimenting with paper collage, fabric, dye, thread and stitching in Textile Design*

wrapping them in fabric for a more rounded effect. The result was successful but she needed to find an appropriate covering material. Nylon seemed to work well and by cutting into the back of the calico, tucking a section from an old pair of tights into the space, padding it and closing the back with hand stitching, a suitably rounded shape could be produced. The technique seemed to work. Isobelle had established a new construction method but initially the colour was wrong. She knew from previous work that dyes were available so she tried mixing a variety of shades and strengths which could be applied to her fabric stones. She produced several samples (Figure 2.17).

Using contextual sources to suggest materials for use in textile experiments

One of the textile artists named on the question paper prompted Isobelle to consider using less conventional materials in her work. Sue Lawty had used stones, shells and pebbles collected from the beach to create precise compositions which complemented her tapestry pieces (Figure 2.18). Isobelle

AQA *Examiner's tip*

You might include swatches of assorted fabric, weights, colours and structures in your preparatory studies. Use small pieces of cloth to try out different strengths of dye; try dye on both wet and dry material for alternative results.

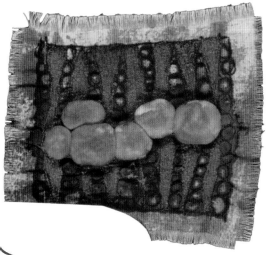

2.17 *Textile experiments; creating a 3D form and exploring dye effects*

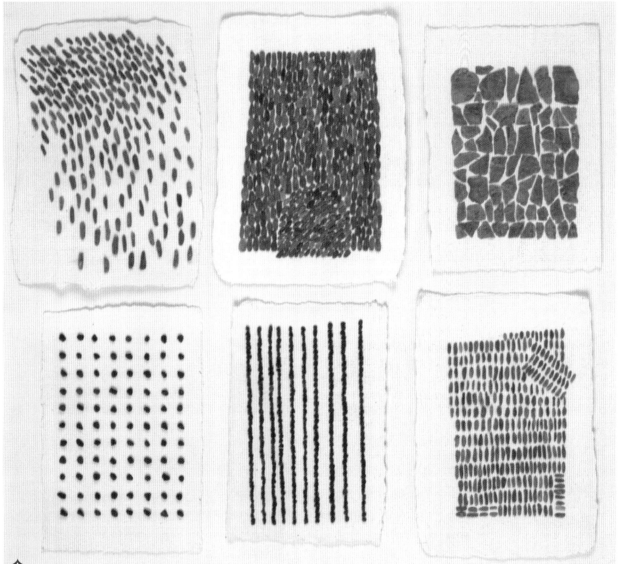

2.18 *Sue Lawty uses stones to create compositions*

wished to experiment with this idea in her own work. She discovered tiny drilled stones which she could stitch onto her fabric. This enabled her to present a contrast of scale between actual stones and her fabric creations (Figure 2.19).

The grid-like structure of the lobster pot was another feature Isobelle wanted to examine. Her understanding of the technique of cut-work suggested it might prove to be a possible medium for translating the patterns revealed by the crossing ropes. By experimenting with layering different types and weights of decorative materials to create a base, stitching a grid over the surface, then cutting away layers to reveal underlying materials, Isobelle was able to use her investigative studies of materials and techniques to help further her intentions (Figure 2.20).

2.20 *Cutwork to explore pattern in Textile Design*

Using materials and techniques to extend ideas and learn new processes

In Case study 17 Isobelle wanted to convey a sense of the beach and 'capture the differences between the shoreline itself, the sea and the sky'. She also demonstrated that in addition to selecting and using appropriate materials and techniques, by experimenting she could:

- extend her knowledge of fabrics and dyes
- develop new methods of working

2.21 *Andy Goldsworthy used stone and wood to create* Stone houses, Digne-Les-Bains, France, 16 June 1995

- develop new techniques
- develop skills
- investigate visual forms.

Isobelle discovered that her understanding of materials and techniques was vital to helping her create the outcome she wanted. She knew that she hoped to include a 3D element to reflect the uneven surface of the beach, but she needed to learn new skills and experiment with materials and processes in order to make this happen. Her preparatory studies document her journey and show how she:

- experimented with fabric weights and layered gauzes, nets, ribbons and calico
- manipulated materials to enable the creation of pebbles
- mastered a braiding foot to twist creative yarns
- experimented with a soldering iron on sheer fabrics and ribbons to explore a contrast of texture
- investigated pattern qualities suggested by a primary resource.

Alternative approaches

More textile experiments

Try creating a new fabric by bonding fibres through felting or melting filaments together with an iron.

Use paper stencils to print shapes and try repeating the image or over-lapping sections of the motif.

Use wax, gutta or a starch paste to block out sections or lines in a design prior to dying.

In Case study 18 Kirsty combined her understanding of materials and techniques and used this knowledge to refine her ideas. Her Portfolio of Work had provided her with opportunities to try new and diverse working methods which then allowed her to demonstrate her understanding of materials during the Externally Set Task.

Remember

When using a warm soldering iron to distort fabrics, place the material to be treated on a non-combustible surface and always work in a well-ventilated area. When bonding fibres together, cover your work with greaseproof paper before ironing.

2.22 *Andy Goldsworthy used leaves and water as his materials in work created in Laumeier Sculpture Park, Missouri, June 1994*

Case study 18

Experimenting with materials and techniques in Graphic Communication

Kirsty responded to an 'issues-based' brief in which she investigated the relationship between words and image. Kirsty produced a series of mounted sheets which demonstrate the development of her final piece through experiments in painting, photography, collage and layering processes. She used a self-portrait as her starting point and considered the content, scale and depiction of words and lettering in relation to it. Her final response is a painted portrait, surrounded by and filled in with text (Figure 2.23).

2.23 *Graphics outcome using words and image*

2.24 *A photographic image with collage*

2.25 *A photographic image with paint*

The resources needed for this piece were suggested by the design brief. The style of text and nature of the image, however, were Kirsty's choice and it was important for her to select appropriate sources. The conventional ideal of beauty was one idea Kirsty wished to consider.

The way that Stefan Sagmeister mixed self-portrait images with overlaid, written comment inspired Kirsty to experiment with paint. Sagmeister had also used shapes suggestive of a reptile's skin superimposed over images and Kirsty felt this was another area she could explore through experimenting with media and techniques.

Kirsty overlaid a black and white transparency of her face onto a collaged background. By photocopying an image of her self-portrait onto acetate sheets and fitting these on top of torn, text-covered, newsprint backgrounds,

2.26 *Combining a photographic image with collage and paint*

Kirsty created compositions that enabled her to develop painting experiments which showed an influence of Sagmeister's technique. She copied one of Sagmeister's paintings to help her understand how he used the scale-like pattern and then tried this effect on one of her acetate sheets (Figure 2.25).

In her copy of the Sagmeister, Kirsty used watercolour but for working on acetate she changed her medium to acrylic. This enabled her to experiment with brushstrokes. Colours could be blended and smudged to create a background or with control to suggest precise shapes. Kirsty investigated how she could use the painting process to refine her ideas and she experimented with paint over single and repeated portrait studies. She tried positive and negative photographs over coloured backgrounds and experimented with layering the collaged text on top of the photograph, then painting the surface (Figure 2.26).

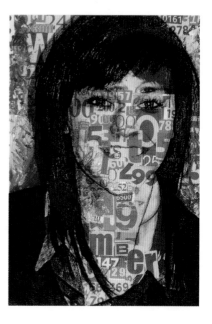

2.27 *Combining text and image*

Kirsty collected cut-out letters and numbers from newspapers, leaflets and magazines and introduced these to her work, again in the form of collages, photocopied acetates and overlaid transparencies. She repeated images to create a sense of pattern and tried painting letter shapes which were similar to the reptile scales of her earlier research. Kirsty experimented with different typefaces and her experiments with media and processes helped her to refine her ideas (Figure 2.27).

Sagmeister had used hand-painted text across his body image and Kirsty hoped her materials could be manipulated to allow her to write in free-hand. She experimented with different consistencies of paint and sizes of brush to find the best technique. Kirsty experimented with different arrangements of text and the direction it would follow around the contours of the face.

Using materials, techniques and processes to explore a specific brief

In Case study 18 Kirsty was able to demonstrate her skills in using

- photography
- collage
- paint.

She had developed a working knowledge of processes and techniques in her Portfolio of Work, but the Externally Set Task enabled her to develop her understanding in experimenting and applying her skills to a specific brief.

In her project, Kirsty considered the illusion of specific images, camouflage and the words we use to describe thoughts and ideas. These were quite complex ideas but they could be associated with particular pictures. Kirsty knew that she could use the skills and techniques developed during the course to help her:

- select appropriate resources
- experiment with composition
- explore depth and scale
- experiment with colour, texture and pattern.

Kirsty discovered that her experiments with media, techniques and processes enabled her to refine her ideas.

- By changing from watercolour to acrylic a different intensity of colour could be created.
- By copying photographs onto acetate sheets compositions could be changed and repeat patterns created.
- Acetate images enabled a layered effect between different types of media.
- Collage could provide ideas for surface quality.
- Text scale and size could vary to create impact.

AQA *Examiner's tip*

Experiment with different scales and styles of lettering in your work. Experiment with:

- collected newspaper text and lettering
- downloaded text
- photocopies which are enlarged or reduced
- acetate sheets to layer images.

Did you know ??????

The artist Jasper Johns used lettering and stencilled numbers in many of his works.

⦶ links

For more examples of ways to combine text and image see Case study 2 in Chapter 1.

2.28 *Barbara Kruger* Untitled *(1982)*

Alternative approaches

Experimenting with materials to depict text

- Paint reversed, photocopied text with Image Maker, leave to dry then wash off the paste.

- Write with wax crayon or oil pastel, brush over with a wash to reveal your text.

- Print lettering or text onto Heat Transfer Paper and then iron onto fabric.

Refining ideas

In all the case studies in this chapter, artists and students discovered that not all the ideas or techniques they used were always successful. Sometimes a colour was too strong, a texture too smooth, paint too thick or a type of paper inappropriate for its purpose. Photographs could be out of focus and plaster or clay could crack while drying. Some experiments needed to be reworked, others needed to be enlarged and in some cases a material proved to be totally unsuitable.

Getting a different result from the one you expected does not always mean that the material or technique that you selected was inappropriate. In a number of the case studies students found samples, maquettes, drawings and paintings could be reviewed and once the results had been considered, improvements could be made. Sometimes, further experiments and refinements in developing a particular technique were needed. In Case study 14, Lauren found that she had to try out different mixtures of bitumen, glue, gesso and sand in order to achieve the most effective texture. She needed the surface to be sticky enough to hold the sand, yet solid enough for her to scratch into. In Case study 17, Isobelle tried a variety of dye strengths and fabric weights in her search for the best way to recreate pebbles with textiles (Figure 2.29). Some fabrics were too thick to pull through the calico while others would not hold the dye. Isobelle tried different experiments with her fabric selection and discovered that nylon worked best.

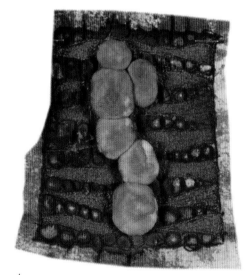
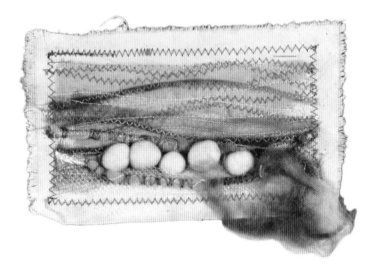

2.29 *Refining materials in Textile Design*

Potter Sarah McCormack finds that she needs to consider how long her pieces take to make when she reviews her experiments in clay. Although she does not find her materials expensive, they are very time consuming to use and she needs to consider this when planning her final designs. Sarah also adapts her designs and refines her ideas as her understanding of the materials develops. As she explores ideas and techniques, she finds the processes which work best and discards others. If a piece is not quite right, she will remove an element, replace it, make an alteration or addition and continue to experiment until she achieves a successful outcome (Figure 2.30).

Using media and techniques to refine ideas as they progress

Discussing your project ideas, use of materials and experimental results with your teacher is always useful.

As you experiment and refine your ideas, you might discover more exciting and unexpected directions for your art work. You may find that a particular medium enables you to investigate and express a specific quality or characteristic of your source material more successfully. For example, drawing with a black biro or fine-line pen may help you to explore the linear quality of a group of objects better than a pencil. This could lead you to experiment with lino printing. By cutting into the lino with different shapes of blade, a variety of thick and thin lines can be created. In Case study 18, Kirsty used acetate images to help refine her compositional ideas. By enlarging her photograph, repeating it and placing it over different backgrounds she could assess the most effective way to develop her paintings.

Elements to consider when refining your work

When reviewing you own work consider how your choice of media and technical ability could help you to refine your ideas. Ask yourself questions about:

- the shape and texture of the surface you are working on
- the relationship between the shapes and forms within a composition or design
- the tonal contrast between dark and light areas
- the range of colours
- the size and scale of shapes and forms
- the amount of detail included.

Think about how you could refine your handling of media to explore your images. You might:

- experiment with different brush sizes and shapes
- apply paint with a knife, rags or your fingers
- tear and cut paper for different qualities of edge
- use Adobe Photoshop to distort, crop, repeat, reverse or manipulate the colour of images
- change the consistency of paint, dye or slip
- make marks lighter, heavier, thicker, thinner, looser or sharper
- rework an image using a different medium such as oil pastel, chalk pastel, ink and wash
- invert the positive and negative spaces
- change from 2D to 3D.

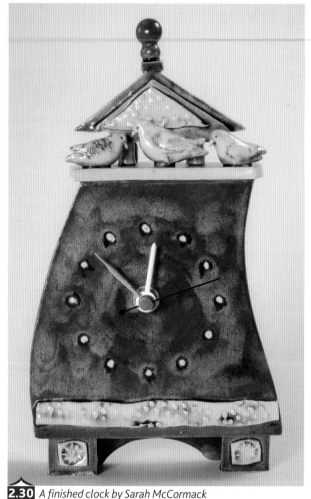

2.30 *A finished clock by Sarah McCormack*

Case study 19

Refining ideas in Photography

In this Externally Set Task Abigail applied her skills in using Adobe Photoshop to refine her ideas in response to the theme of 'Identity'. She produced a series of digital contact prints and manipulated photographic images.

Abigail considered how three artists approached the theme of identity: Richard Avedon's portraits, Cindy Sherman's portrayal of women, and how Barbara Kruger has mixed images with words and phrases.

Richard Avedon's prints inspired her to look deeper than the surface portrait and think about things that make up a person's identity, such as blood cells and fingerprints. Abigail began to realise that photography did not always need to be presented in true natural colour or black and white. She wanted to experiment with colour and how it could suggest personality within a portrait.

Abigail took a series of digital portrait images which were manipulated in Adobe Photoshop. She took photographs of things people liked and experimented with layering these with images of faces and fingerprints. She adjusted the colours and experimented with contrasting tones. Strong colour contrasts worked best and Abigail found that these helped her express the personality of her model. Using appropriate techniques, Abigail experimented with composition and colour, and printed them as small images for further reflection, and refinement (Figure 2.31). She selected the images she wanted to work with and made further refinements to them. Textures were introduced, exaggerated, softened, saved or rejected, patterns highlighted or reduced, and features emphasised.

Did you know

Cindy Sherman used images from old master paintings and films of the 1950s to create works with a documentary style. Her recent work uses digital manipulation to question themes of female stereotype as well as social concepts.

AQA Examiner's tip

Use a bold pen to mark or highlight contact prints to show how you selected particular photographic images for further refinement or development.

Remember

Consider the weight and quality of paper that you use for printing photographs and digital images.

 2.31 *Abigail's contact prints*

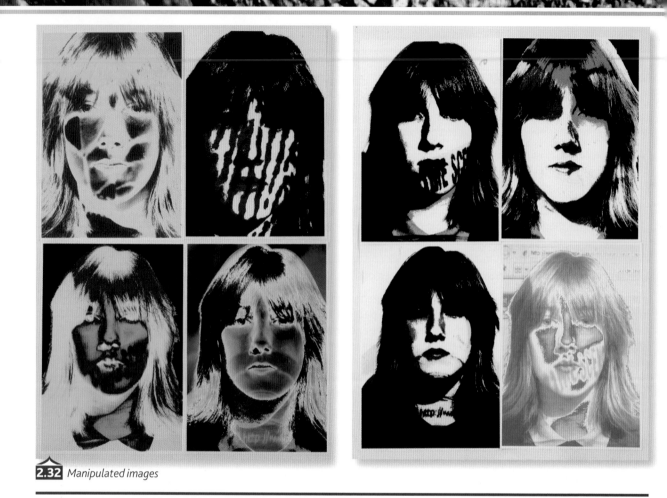

2.32 *Manipulated images*

Using digital media to refine ideas

When using digital media and traditional darkroom techniques for black and white or colour photography it is important to show how you have refined your ideas as they progress. Storyboards, test strips, contact prints, annotated trial prints and desktop or computer screengrabs can help show how you have developed and refined your images and ideas. In Case study 19, Abigail presented a selection of small scale printouts which demonstrate how she manipulated her first portrait pictures through a series of stages in which she explored layering and experimented with colours. In Case study 14, Lauren experimented with Adobe Photoshop to refine and manipulate the contrast in her digital images (Figure 2.4). In both case studies the students found that by thinking about the results they achieved in their experiments, they could develop their skills and refine their ideas.

To help you refine your ideas using digital media, you might experiment with:

- manipulating images using Adobe Photoshop or other software programs
- selecting the composition by cropping images or using the zoom
- changing the contrast of tone or brightness of colour
- combining images by layering
- editing to remove specific areas.

If using a camera, you might consider how your images could be refined by:

- changing the shutter speed
- varying the depth of field
- using the zoom or changing the lens
- using filters
- adjusting the lighting
- applying tones or tints during processing
- adjusting the exposure during printing.

Case study 20

Refining ideas in Textile Design

Isobel used her experience of living in Africa for four years to select appropriate resources in response to an Externally Set Task based on 'African Tradition'. She produced an A3 sketchbook which includes reflections of her time in Nigeria, photographs of artefacts she had collected, swatches of traditional fabrics, experiments with dyes and stitching, and sketches of patterns for woodblock prints and batik. During the 10-hour period of supervised time she produced

 African fabrics provide inspiration for colour and pattern

kerboodle!

a fabric panel which combined a number of textile processes and illustrated an understanding of African design.

Isobel selected material from a diverse range of sources that included wooden sculptures, paintings, masks, beads and fabric. She used pencil to draw several of the masks that she had collected (Figure 2.34). She thought about their ritual significance, how they are different from tribe to tribe, and how fabrics differ between cultural regions. Pencil drawings enabled Isobel to experiment with and to develop compositional ideas in which she mixed patterns together to produce more complex images.

Isobel sketched out a variety of design plans and decided that she wanted to assemble blocks of pattern to create a more intense image. However her knowledge of textile processes led her to believe that it would be too difficult to fit different blocks together and her work would be more successful if she could rotate and piece one image instead of several (Figure 2.35). Isobel wanted to find out how a simplified design would work on fabric. She experimented with dye strengths, reviewed her colours and refined their tonal values. At first she thought that orange and purple would work, but after reviewing her samples discovered that she needed to introduce a navy blue. This worked well and allowed her to focus on techniques. She cut a wood block, used it to print with, and experimented with batik.

2.34 *Drawing of an African Mask*

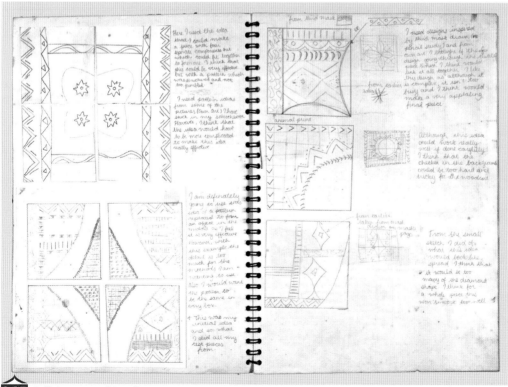

2.35 *Refining compositions for a repeat pattern*

∞links

See Chapter 1 for more about using contextual material.

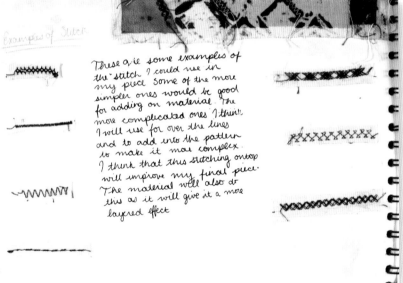

These are some examples of the stitch I could use in my piece. Some of the more simpler ones would be good for adding on material. The more complicated ones I think I will use for over the lines and to add into the pattern to make it more complex. I think that this stitching ontop will improve my final piece. The material will also do this as it will give it a more layered effect

2.36 *A woodblock print to refine dyeing options and stitching effects*

Isobel decided that she could refine her work by adding stitching to enhance the pattern quality and to exaggerate the vertical lines and diamond shapes frequently found on African textiles (Figure 2.36). She experimented with machine stitching techniques, and chose simple stitches as she felt more complex ones could make her work look too cluttered. Isobel photographed her print samples and used downloaded images as a ground for more stitch experiments (Figure 2.37). These allowed her to refine pattern details for her final composition (Figure 2.38).

2.37 *Refining stitching effects*

2.38 *Final textile panel*

Alternative approaches

Exploring African Art through textile media

■ Use vegetables such as potatoes to cut simple block patterns.

■ Use a paste made from flour and water to investigate Nigerian starch resist fabrics.

■ Bunch, pleat or fold fabric; then bind tightly with string. Dip into coloured dye and, once dry, remove the string to reveal patterns.

Selecting, experimenting and refining

Isobel found that in selecting and experimenting with appropriate resources, media, techniques and processes, she could refine her ideas. Isobel learned that:

■ memories and experiences helped her in the selection of appropriate resources

■ experimenting with compositions helped her to decide which designs would translate into batik and block prints

■ taking a rubbing from a woodblock can suggest the depth of cut and help to refine the design

- samples of dye experiments can help to refine colour and tone
- experiments can help to refine the selection of materials and processes
- photographs of her samples helped to refine her ideas.

Using your discoveries in media, materials, techniques and processes

In each case study in this chapter, the students found that their understanding of resources, media, and materials was important to the development and production of their art work. Not every student had access to the same resources or chose to use the same techniques, but they shared an enthusiasm to explore and experiment. Each developed their understanding of the properties and characteristics of different materials and techniques, and experimented with them to discover the effects they could achieve.

Remember to consider the following points to help you succeed.

- Develop your understanding of media, processes and techniques.
- Select appropriate resources, media and techniques to refine your ideas.
- Experiment with new skills and approaches.
- Make time for the development of skills.
- Review your experiments and question your results.
- Refine your ideas and try making changes.
- Enjoy the creative process!

Learning outcomes

Having read this chapter you should now be able to:

develop your knowledge of media, materials, techniques and processes

select and identify appropriate resources, media, materials, techniques and processes

develop skills in using media and techniques

explore and experiment with ideas using appropriate techniques and processes

demonstrate how you can use materials and processes to refine your ideas.

Objectives

In this chapter you will learn how to:

record your ideas, observations and insights

record the development of your work

use digital media for recording observations and ideas.

Recording is the process of collecting information in visual, written and other forms, and providing evidence of your ideas, observations and insights. Throughout your Art and Design work you will record ideas, make observations and document your insights and intentions. This may be done in different ways. You will work from different types of experiences and source materials, and these may lead to different ways of developing your ideas. You will also need to reflect upon your work as it progresses, thinking about what you have achieved at each stage, and what you will do next.

3.1 *Frida Kahlo* What the Water Gave Me *(1938)*

AQA Examiner's tip

Use a range of appropriate materials, working methods and approaches when recording your ideas, insights and intentions.

Recording is a process that involves:

- recording your ideas in visual and other forms which might include 'new media' such as digital or video processes
- making observations from **primary sources** or direct experience, or by using **secondary sources** as inspiration, for example, images of artefacts, objects, people, places or events
- working from your own memories or recollections
- recording or documenting your insights into images and experiences in your practical work. For example by making studies or samples of techniques, drawings or sketches of layouts, compositions or designs
- recording your intentions as you develop your ideas. For example, you might explore the possibilities of using different colours, viewpoints or designs
- developing the skills to **reflect** on your work and consider how you might progress to the next stage of a project

Many artists, craftspeople and designers have found it useful to keep a sketchbook as a developing collection of observations, ideas, insights and intentions (Figure 3.2).

You will need to present your work in an organised way, so that your understanding, intentions and ideas are clear. Studies, drawings, maquettes, photographs, diagrams, written and other material could be gathered together in sketchbooks, **journals** or **logs**, as well as being presented as a portfolio, a slide or digital presentation, or mounted sheets of studies.

Key terms

Primary sources: source material that you can study directly from first-hand experience, for example a still-life group in the art room, a performance, working in a landscape or from a painting in a gallery.

Secondary sources: reproductions of images and artefacts, music, text, poetry, film – source material that is produced by others.

Reflect: to look back at your work and think about how it has progressed, in relation to your intentions.

Journal: a collection of information about technical data, techniques and processes, and reflections on contextual material relevant to the development of your work.

Log: a diary, both written and visual that usually relates to an event or experience such as a workshop or gallery visit.

3.2 *Henry Moore* Drawing for Sculpture *(1940) (HMF1484)*

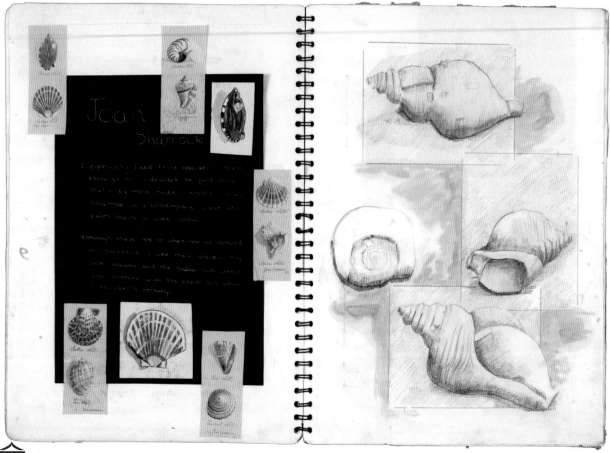

3.3 Sketchbook page

The recording of ideas might be evident in your work in different ways.

You might choose to record your first responses to a starting point or brief in sketches, drawings, photographs or diagrams, perhaps supported by jottings or notes. You might make a mind map or use a similar technique to help you to think about and record possible ideas and the different ways that you might approach a theme, issue or brief.

You might provide a record of your first ideas by collecting and selecting images that are appropriate to your intentions. You might do fieldwork that could include taking photographs or making drawings.

Remember

You should select appropriate media and processes for your recording to be effective.

AQA **Examiner's tip**

Present your work so that your ideas and intentions are clear.

Case study 21

Recording ideas in Photography

Elizabeth has responded to an Externally Set Task starting point entitled 'Detail'. This Photography project is presented in three A3 sketchbooks which contain both digital and traditional black and white processed images.

Elizabeth's work provides a record of her ideas in exploring detail in the natural environment. Her observations are recorded using a disposable camera loaded with colour film, digital images and black and white printing. Contact sheets provide evidence of Elizabeth recording her investigation of various viewpoints

3.4 *Photographs showing different viewpoints*

and different subjects including rock formations, cliffs and beaches, fruit, flowers and organic textures such as bark, pine cones and sawn wood (Figure 3.4).

In the second sketchbook, Elizabeth has explored these subjects in more depth. She has recorded how appropriate contextual material has informed her ideas, by presenting some of her own images alongside examples of works by other photographers and artists.

In recording her observations of changing light and weather conditions, Elizabeth demonstrates her technical understanding. Her close-ups of flowers record connections Elizabeth has made with the ideas in Georgia O'Keeffe's abstract works (see Figure 3.5).

Elizabeth's photographs are a record of her ideas. Her photographs are carefully selected, composed and presented in order to record these connections explaining connections between her work and that of others, including Karl Blossfeldt, Edward Weston and Georgia O'Keeffe. Also there are some clear annotations which record Elizabeth's technical understanding and the influences on the development of her ideas.

3.5 *Sketchbook page*

Key terms

Photogram: a photograph produced by using an object instead of a negative in the darkroom. A method used by Louis Daguerre and Man Ray.

Remember

Digital and electronic media are valuable resources for:

- recording ideas and observations
- recording the development of your ideas
- documenting your work
- demonstrating different ideas and approaches.

3.6 *A photogram*

Recording to develop your ideas

As you begin to develop an understanding of an idea, theme, issue or brief, you should record your observations and insights from your sources, to provide yourself with material and information for the development of your ideas. These thoughts and observations might be in the form of sketches, studies, drawings, colour studies, or they might be images in which you analyse your source material, record experiments with materials, techniques and processes, or you might record your response to contextual material by making studies or notes that analyse relevant aspects of appropriate works by other artists, designers and craftspeople.

You might record your observations in other ways, using film, video, sound or recordings of performances to inform the development of your ideas.

AQA **Examiner's tip**

When recording your ideas, experiment with appropriate media and techniques.

∞ **links**

See Chapter 1 for more about contextual and other sources.

See Chapter 1 for more about investigating and developing ideas.

See Chapter 2 for more about experimenting with materials, techniques and processes.

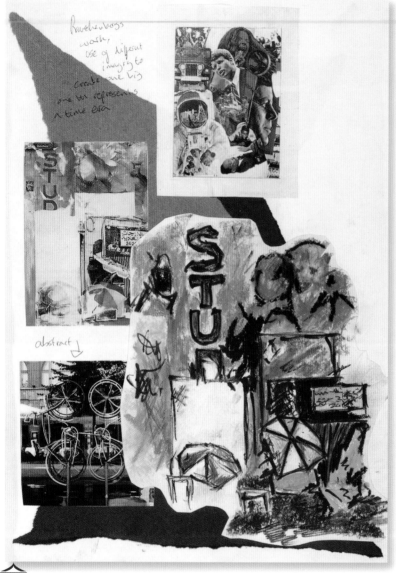

3.7 *Sketchbook page recording source images*

Case study 22

A designer recording ideas in Graphic Communication

Air is a professional design agency based in Cheltenham. The professional presentation in this case study includes preliminary design ideas and a six-page brochure produced for a personnel company called *Red 10*. When recording the client's requirements the designers working for Air:

▥ make notes

▥ sketch out ideas using a layout pad with marker pen or pencil.

Ideas are recorded back at the studio rather than directly in front of a client, unless it is necessary to discuss something like the possible format of a folded brochure.

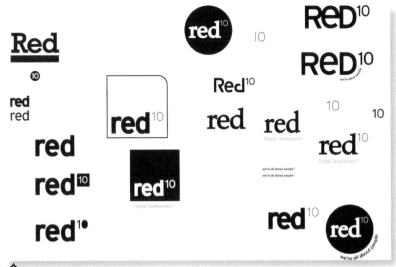

3.8 *Air logo ideas for Red 10*

The recording of initial ideas is usually in the form of rough sketches rather than polished, finished drawings. Ideas and finished designs are worked up using computer software such as Adobe Illustrator for a logo, or Adobe Indesign for a publication such as a brochure or annual report. Occasionally, if Air designers have a particularly clear vision of the concept, they will start recording ideas using the computer without sketching it out first (Figure 3.7).

Most clients now expect to see ideas recorded and presented in an almost finished format. Air normally present more than one concept and, for example, if the brief is for a corporate identity, there might be up to four logo design proposals, each of which will be printed and mounted for presentation to the client. Any amendments that are required are recorded directly onto these.

Recording the development of ideas

Your work should provide evidence or a record of how your ideas have developed, the ways in which you have explored alternatives and refined your ideas. You might do this through a series of studies or images that show the ways in which you have developed a personal response to your source material, the ways in which you have explored and refined alternative compositions, designs or layouts, or have developed a three-dimensional form or construction.

Contact prints and test strips in photography, samplers or experiments with dyes, stitches or materials in textiles, or screen grabs in graphics might provide a record of the way that you have developed ideas. You might make a photographic or video record of the progress of a piece of three-dimensional work (see Figure 3.9 and Case study 27).

Your work might, in a purely practical way, provide a record of the development of your ideas but, where it is appropriate, you could also choose to support your practical work with annotations alongside images, or by including a sound recording on a video. Rather than just describing your work, record the development of your ideas by analysing or **evaluating** what you have done.

> **Remember**
>
> If you choose to annotate your work, your comments should be analytical.

> **Key terms**
>
> **Evaluate:** to look back, reflecting on the strengths and weaknesses of an idea or image, comparing ideas or images and making a judgement or decision.

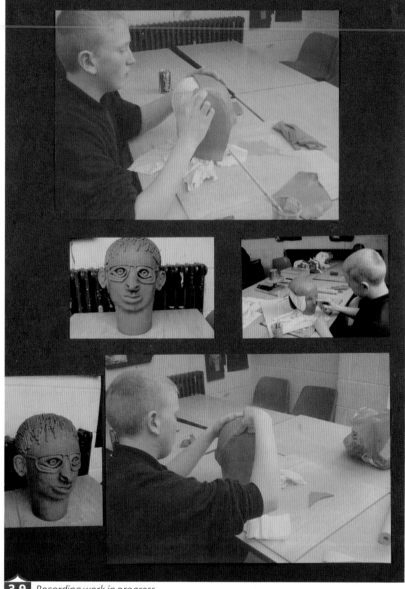

3.9 *Recording work in progress*

Recording ideas might include:

- responses to a starting point, an idea, issue, theme or brief
- ideas and alternatives you have considered
- mind maps or mood boards
- responses to the ideas of other artists, designers or craftspeople
- the development of your response to source material
- ideas generated or developed from experimentation with materials, techniques and processes
- stages in the development and refinement of an idea, composition, design or layout
- maquettes or models.

3.10 *Recording observations*

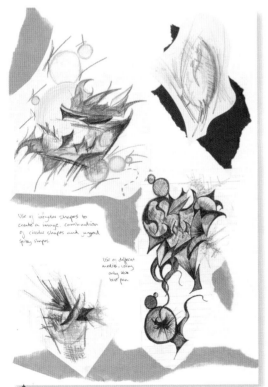

3.11 *Recording ideas*

Recording ideas in Graphic Communication

Acheson has responded to an Externally Set Task starting point on the theme of 'Distortion'. He has presented his work in an A3 sketchbook in which he has recorded his ideas and observations in various media, including pen, pencil, pastel, collage and photography. The development of Acheson's ideas has been informed by Georgia O'Keeffe, Robert Rauschenberg, Pop Art and contemporary graffiti artists: (see Figure 3.12).

Acheson's response to a series of motifs and logo designs from the music industry demonstrate the way that Acheson has recorded ideas (see Figure 3.13). He also organises his own studies carefully alongside secondary source images to help record connections between his own ideas and the ways in which the artists have:

- explored visual elements such as composition, space and colour
- used various processes, working methods and techniques
- communicated ideas and meanings.

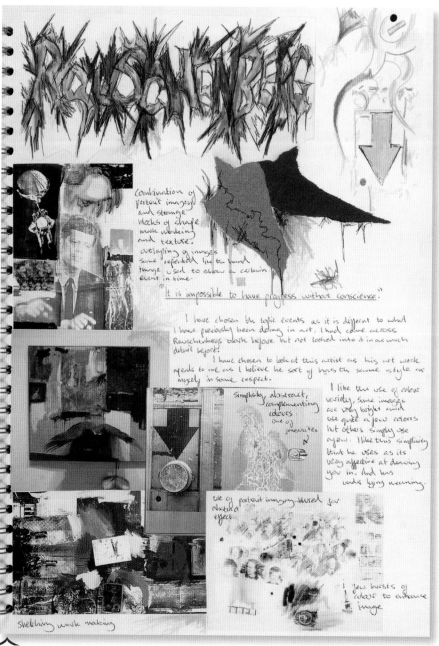

3.12 *Recording ideas from a contextual source – Rauschenberg*

3.13 *Examples of letter forms in sketchbook*

Recording observations

Your observations can be recorded in many different ways and you should choose media, materials and techniques that are appropriate to your area of study and to your intentions. You might record using drawing and painting media, photographic, digital or electronic media, textiles media, sculptural or construction materials. Observations can be recorded in an entirely practical way, for example, through drawing and painting, using lens- or light-based media, through still or motion images, in collecting and selecting surfaces and textures. They can also, where appropriate, be supported by sound recordings, the spoken word or in written form.

> **AQA** *Examiner's tip*
>
> Select appropriate materials, processes and techniques when recording your observations.

Recording observations using drawing

Drawing can take many different forms. They can be loose, spontaneous sketches and drawings that are made quickly, recording your observations on location or from a subject that is moving. These are a kind of shorthand, a simplification, a way of making visual notes. Sketches and drawings like these can help to record your first reactions to source material and can also enable you to record information and observations quickly.

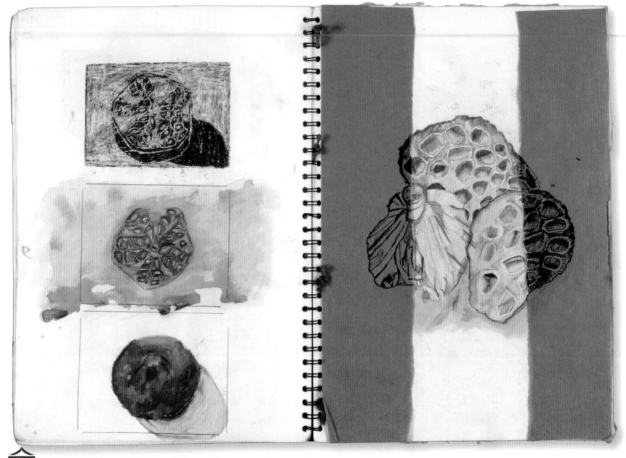

3.14 *Recording observations using different drawing techniques*

Drawings and colour studies can also take much longer and be more sustained, more thorough and analytical in nature. These are studies in which you look hard and in depth at your source material. You might explore and record your observations of particular characteristics of tone, form, colour or texture, for example, or elements such as light, weather and atmosphere.

If you were working from the human figure, you might make quick, loose sketches of groupings of figures in a public space, or capture the figure in motion, but you might also make longer, more sustained studies in which, for example, you look closely and record your observations in a portrait or a character study of the static, posed figure.

There are other ways of recording your observations in different forms of drawing. Working with lens- or light-based media, selecting and framing an image into a composition is, effectively, a form of drawing. In a similar way, observations can be recorded using materials to draw with, such as stitch, wire, clay, cut and torn paper, and fabrics.

Drawing can also provide ways of recording observations and insights in your investigations of the work of artists, designers and craftspeople. Where appropriate, studies in monochrome and in colour can help you to look at and to understand how a work uses formal elements, a particular medium or technique, how an artist has responded to an idea or location, or how a designer has responded to a brief or a design problem.

⬭links

See Chapter 1 for more about using contextual material.

3.15 *Drawings in different media*

3.16 *Max Ernst* The Forest *(1927)*

Recording observations in Graphic Communication

Acheson's 'Distortion' project includes drawings in a range of media and photographs which record his observations of objects in a jar of water, with a focus on swirls, reflections and distortions. His observations are recorded using materials such as:

- torn papers
- crayons
- wire
- pen

to record the visual qualities of the forms, shapes and distortions, and the excitement and vitality Acheson has seen in them (Figure 3.17).

3.17 *Recording observations and ideas*

Alternative approaches

Instead of recording from first-hand experience, you could collect secondary source images related to a theme such as 'reflections in water and glass'.

You could:

- set up a still life of shiny objects, recording observations in drawings or with a camera

- drop different inks or dyes in water and draw or photograph with a digital or video camera

- record from different reflective surfaces in the local environment such as shop windows, car bodywork or puddles

- record observations close-up, using the 'macro' setting on a digital camera

- manipulate your images using Adobe Photoshop: try altering colours, smudging, cloning or repeating sections.

3.18 *Janet Fish* Plastic Boxes *(2007)*

(www.artnet.com)

Artists, designers and craftspeople draw in different ways to record their ideas and make observations. Give yourself time to develop and refine your observational skills and your skills in handling materials, processes and techniques to record your ideas, observations and intentions successfully.

Drawing may be used in a variety of ways to record ideas, observations and insights. Through drawing you can:

- observe and record from first- and second-hand experience

- analyse and record your observations of images, objects, artefacts and environments, making sketches and drawings that emphasise elements such as line, shape, tone, form, scale, texture and colour

Remember

There are a number of ways to record your observations:

- by making quick sketches
- by making **analytical studies**
- by using different materials, techniques and processes

Key terms

Analytical studies: studies that analyse source material in depth.

AQA *Examiner's tip*

Work at developing and refining your skills – your drawing, painting, modelling or other skills – to help you record your ideas, observations and intentions successfully.

⬭ links

See Chapter 2 for more about developing skills.

- record how you will produce something on a larger scale, in a different medium or material
- record the development of your ideas through studies that show alternative compositions, designs or layouts and how you have refined your ideas
- record the development and refinement of ideas through experimenting with materials, techniques and processes
- analyse and record your observations of the work of other artists, designers and craftspeople.

⬭links

See Chapter 2 for more about refining ideas and experimenting with materials, techniques and processes.

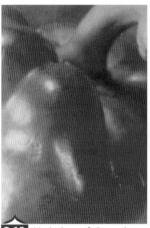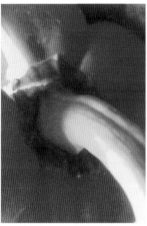

3.19 *Variations of viewpoint and composition*

3.20 *Tonal study in charcoal from still life*

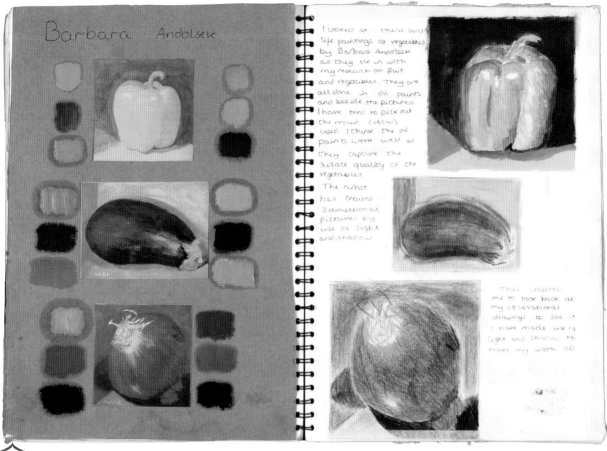

3.21 *Studies recording personal response to an artist*

Case study 25

A designer recording observations in Graphic Communication

Before designing signage, a digital camera is used to record the features of the intended site or location. The photo image is then used to demonstrate how a sign will look by superimposing the design onto the photo using Adobe Photoshop. This 'visual' is presented to the client for approval before the sign is printed.

The most successful idea is often applied to several design contexts for presentation to the client. For example:

- a brochure cover
- a business card
- a website.

This 'contextualisation' is a very important part of the recording process as it presents to the client a demonstration of how concepts might work in the market place. See Figure 3.22 for a brochure cover design mock-up.

If a client requires a certain style of photography, Air might source contextual examples using an online image library and present these with the brief to the photographer.

3.22 *Brochure cover mock-up*

Recording from direct observation

Working from direct observation can provide you with opportunities to record:

- from different viewpoints, angles and perspectives
- details of surface texture
- a sense of scale and space in relation to surroundings or nearby objects
- form, mass and volume
- subtleties of colour or tone which may be influenced by changing light conditions
- details of construction or structure in natural and manufactured objects
- how materials have been used by manufacturers, designers or artists and craftspeople
- light and atmosphere.

Recording from secondary sources

Working from secondary sources such as photographs or images in books or from the internet can provide you with opportunities to record:

- material that might not otherwise be available to you
- objects or experiences which cannot be readily seen with the naked eye
- historical events or personalities
- places, people or events beyond your immediate experience: different countries, groups, cultures, traditions and belief systems
- artefacts, designs, constructions and works of art and craft which are not readily accessible to you.

Recording observations using photography

The camera can be useful for recording observations and for resourcing work. If you choose photography as a means of recording and observing, you need to remember to show selection and control. It can be easy to point a digital camera at a subject and simply print off the resulting picture but you should:

- demonstrate skills in selecting and framing your subject
- demonstrate your ability to explore the elements of visual language: line, tone, form, colour, pattern and texture.

Photography is about controlling:

- composition
- colour and contrast
- focus
- lighting.

When selecting a subject, look carefully at the colours in the scene or object and consider how these will look in the final print. Similarly try to judge from the lighting conditions whether there will be strong shadows or soft tones throughout the picture; will it be dark or light overall; is the main subject going to be clear or will it be lost in a pattern of surrounding colours or tones?

AQA **Examiner's tip**

Show that you have been selective when taking photographs, and that you have controlled exposure and focus.

Did you know ???????

Digital cameras have only become readily available in the last ten years. Before that, photographers mainly used traditional film and darkroom processes.

Case study 26

Recording observations in Photography

In response to the theme of 'Detail', Elizabeth's early photographs provide a visual record of her search for a subject and an idea. She considered not only the content of the images, but also the technical challenges of different locations and subjects. The problems and challenges of photographing textures in low light conditions and the issues of backlighting and exposure posed by branches silhouetted against the sky are recorded in visual form (Figure 3.24).

Inspired by Blossfeldt, O'Keeffe and Weston, Elizabeth recorded her observations in a series of studies of close-ups of fruit, plant stems and vegetables. Her images record the ways that she explored different viewpoints, focus and compositions (again, Figure 3.24).

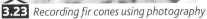
3.23 *Recording fir cones using photography*

Studies of bark and wood grain in different light and additional images of fir cones (Figure 3.23) provide a record of Elizabeth developing her ideas and her understanding of depth of field, focus and lighting.

3.24 *Recording observations from natural forms*

When recording you could explore:

- carefully selected viewpoints
- interesting vantage points
- low angles
- close-ups for recording contrasting surfaces (Figure 3.26).

These are all important parts of the language of image making, and your observations should show you have considered these whenever possible. Sometimes viewpoints, framing and focus can be experimented with in order to create a more stylised, expressive or atmospheric image (Figure 3.27). For example, the use of the extreme angles and viewpoints can be used to suggest a personal or subjective point of view (Figure 3.28).

3.25 *Similar subjects taken in different light, from different viewpoints*

3.26 *Recording contrasting surface qualities*

3.27 *Bill Brandt* Portrait of a Young Girl, Eaton Place *(1955)*

Lighting is also important in photography. The time of day, seasons and weather all influence how a scene or object appears to us. Control of the patterns or play of light and tonal range in a photo requires a strong understanding of camera controls: shutter speed, aperture and the uses of flash are dealt with at length in a wide range of technical manuals on both film and digital photography.

3.28 *Ernst Haas* Time Life Building *(1955)*

Remember

Important skills when taking photographs include:

- careful framing of your subject matter
- selective focusing
- controlled exposure
- control of colour and contrast.

Case study 27

Recording observations in Three-Dimensional Design

Luke has responded to an Externally Set Task starting point entitled 'Portraits'. He produced two sculpted heads in response to his research. One piece is a traditional portrait, the other a design based on ethnic styles. There are seven mounted research sheets.

Luke used a digital camera to record his observations of the human head and also to record and document the progress of his three-dimensional work. The manipulation of photos is an effective way of visualising distortion of proportions, hair style and personal appearance (Figure 3.29). An early interest and focus on sculpture is recorded on mounted sheets of pictures of contemporary ceramic heads and busts by Glenys Barton (Figure 3.30).

Luke's investigation of the set theme is inspired by his coursework study of Gormley. He recorded that the surface and colour of sculpted forms became a particular interest. The use of filters to develop the colours and textures in his photos makes a connection to the glazes and surface qualities of Barton's works (Figure 3.31).

Luke also recorded his intentions to follow Barton's working principles of using portrait images as inspiration, and to allow his ideas and the identity of his sculpted head to develop as it was constructed. Photographs that

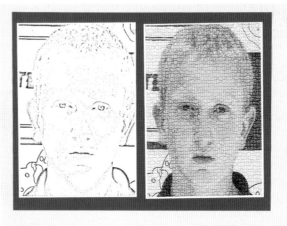

3.29 *Recording different possibilities using digital images*

3.30 *Research sheet on contemporary sculpture*

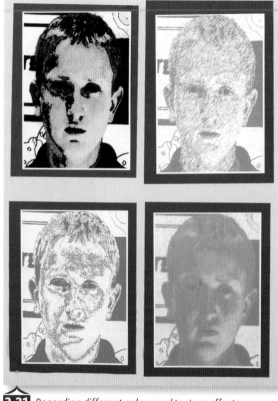
3.31 *Recording different colour and texture effects*

record Luke working are presented on an additional sheet (Figure. 3.9).

The final ceramic forms demonstrate his observational skills when working from primary and secondary sources. The naturalistic head is a good example of 'drawing in clay' and the more stylised, abstract version records connections to his contextual research (Figure 3.32).

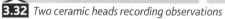
3.32 *Two ceramic heads recording observations*

Case study 28

Recording observations in Fine Art

Lisa responded to an Externally Set Task starting point entitled 'Everyday Objects'. Her work includes an A3 sketchbook containing about 25 pages of studies leading to a final painting in acrylics and watercolour (Figure 3.33).

Lisa recorded her observations and insights into Cubism with printouts of works by Picasso, Braque, Dali and Anthony Armstrong accompanying her own studies from a selection of their works. In these studies she has communicated her understanding of the artists' working methods, with insights into composition, the concept of 'flattened' spaces and forms, and their use of colour.

She made studies which record her observation of still-life groups and demonstrate her understanding of Analytical and Synthetic Cubism.

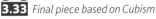 *Final piece based on Cubism*

kerboodle!

3.34 *Picasso* Seated Nude *(1909–10)*

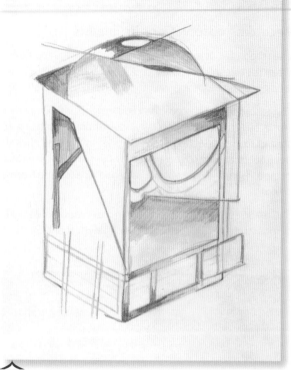

3.36 *Study of a lantern*

3.35 *Study for painting*

Case study 29

Recording observations in Art and Design

Kate has developed a project on the theme of 'Natural Forms'. It includes a series of studies on 25 pages of an A4 sketchbook and a painting in acrylics.

Kate recorded her ideas and insights in visual form, employing a range of techniques and media to record her observations of natural forms, shells, shellfish and seed pods. Surface textures and colours are recorded using pencil, pen, crayon and watercolour, as well as mixed media methods such as **sgraffito** and collage (Figure 3.38).

Pattern, structure and form have been observed, analysed and recorded in Kate's studies.

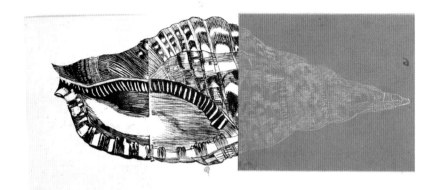

3.37 *Observation of shells inspired by Haeckel*

Key terms

Sgraffito: scratching through an upper layer of colour to reveal the colour or surface beneath (a technique often used in ceramics).

3.38 *Mixed media studies of shells*

3.39 *Final painting based on natural forms*

kerboodle!

Recording insights and intentions

In recording ideas and observations from experiences, from your source materials and from looking at and investigating appropriate works by other artists, designers and craftspeople, you should develop your understanding of ideas, materials, processes and techniques. Your engagement with ideas, processes and with your source material should provide you with insights into the sources that you are working with and into the creative process itself. Insights come from developing your understanding of:

- ideas, themes, issues and starting points
- the nature of your source material
- materials, processes and techniques
- the work of other artists, designers and craftspeople
- the creative process and developing ideas.

Your work should reflect and record the insights you have gained from developing your understanding through investigation, development and experimentation. Your insights should be evident in your practical work but if you include annotations these too should demonstrate your understanding and insights by being more than a descriptive commentary.

Case study 30, Recording Insights in Photography, shows how Elizabeth looked at the work of other artists and photographers to inform her approach to recording from elements within nature. She has demonstrated insight in the understanding shown in her own work and in making clear connections between her work and theirs in the way that she has related one image to another (Figure 3.40).

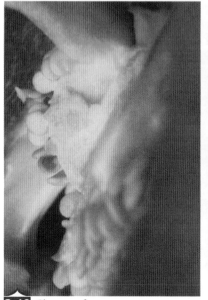 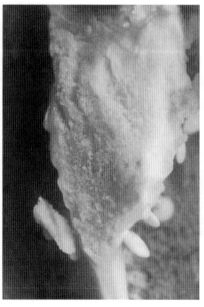 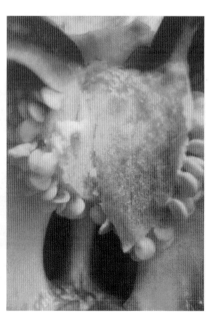

3.40 *Close-ups from peppers*

As your work on a project develops, it should provide evidence of your intentions as your studies record the process of your investigation and the development of your ideas. Your work should form a record of your intentions:

- the slant or focus of your investigation
- your idea, composition or design
- the materials, processes and techniques you intend using
- the way in which you intend to realise your intentions.

Case study 30

Recording insights in Photography

Elizabeth's digital photos of rocks, sand and seaweed at Hengistbury Head record her observations and insights in exploring ideas and developing her intentions relating to composition, viewpoint and deep focus.

Elizabeth's insights into Weston's work on organic forms are recorded in a series of macro shots in which she connects the surface textures of bark, bananas and leaves, emphasising similarities in colour and structure by the careful positioning of images side by side.

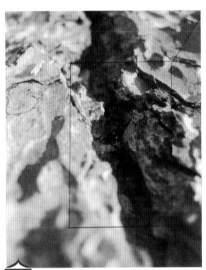
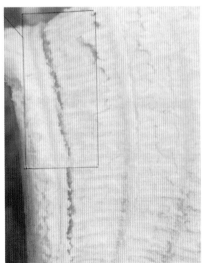

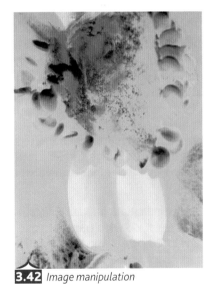

3.41 *Emphasis on similarities in colour and structure*

3.42 *Image manipulation*

The bright colours of Pop Art provided Elizabeth with insights that she recorded in digitally manipulating the hue and saturation of images of peppers.

Some shots of magnolia flowers and roses show Elizabeth taking the opportunity of good natural lighting conditions and carefully selecting her subject. Contextual links are recorded by placing images of roses alongside printouts of O'Keeffe's paintings, and together these record Elizabeth's insights into abstract composition (Figure 3.43).

Elizabeth's insights and intentions are recorded effectively.

3.43 *Abstract compositions from roses*

3.44 *Abstract photograph inspired by O'Keeffe*

Using digital and electronic media for recording

Digital and electronic media are used extensively in Art and Design. Digital photography is used not only by photography students but is frequently used as a medium in other areas of study, as a means of recording observations from source material, or as a sketchbook tool for gathering, collecting and recording visual information. Recording observations and insights through the lens is an integral part of photography, whether using a still camera, film or video.

Electronic media and computer software programs are used for a wide range of purposes such as developing ideas and for the presentation of work, but are also used to record observations and insights, especially in areas of study such as:

- animation, packaging design, design and layout, and illustration
- light-based media.

In Graphic Communication, digital and electronic media are used to record the manipulation of images, typography and layouts and to record the process of investigation, experimentation and development. In Photography, they are used to record the manipulation and processing of images, and in Textile Design, software can be used to record observations about colour, tone, texture and pattern, and to record alternative colourways.

3.45 *Image inspired by Bacon*

In Three-Dimensional Design, software is used to produce visuals and, especially in product design and theatre-set design, it can be used to develop ideas and to record the development process.

Where digital media are used, decisions, observations and insights are often recorded in the form of screen grabs and contact prints. In Photography and in Graphic Communication, observations and insights can be recorded in an electronic sketchbook. Film, video and electronic media can be used to synthesise sound and image.

Recording in other forms

You might use annotations to explain connections between images and ideas, or record initial and developed responses to what you have seen or experienced. These insights might be brought together in a log, journal, storyboard or sketchbook along with collections of related images or studies (Figure 3.47).

Some students make use of a photo-journal in which they record or document the process of making a piece. For example in Case study 27, Luke included photographs of himself working on his clay heads as a response to his research into Barton's ceramic works.

3.46 *Design inspired by Klimt*

⬯links

For more about digital and electronic media see Chapter 1, Chapter 2 and Chapter 4.

3.47 *Studies on the theme of 'Distortion' for Graphic Communication*

A designer recording in Graphic Communication

It is important to record the stages of a design's development and where and how refinements might be made to:

- colour
- tonality
- composition and layout
- typography
- images.

Once refinements are added, 'Air' make the final design into a 'mock-up' for the final presentation to the client. With a brochure this not only gives the client a good idea of the final product but also allows for checking the pagination and makes it easier to proofread (see Figure 3.48).

 3.48 *Brochure page layout for client*

Recording in other forms could include sound, film, video and, where appropriate, written material.

- Screen grabs are a useful way of recording the stages in creating and manipulating a digital image or design (Figure 3.49).
- Draft printouts of images or designs are a good way of recording observations and insights in the design or development process.

- Recording the manipulation of typography, images and layouts is useful in Graphic Communication
- Samplers in Textiles can record different colour combinations, fabrics, techniques or design possibilities.
- A set of maquettes can record ideas or stages in the development of 3D pieces.
- Screen, lino or mono-prints are a good way of recording observations and insights at different stages of development.

Also in sketchbooks or on sheets of studies you could record your insights and intentions through:

- alternative compositions or designs
- working drawings
- experiments with media, processes and techniques
- and, in Photography, recording technical details, speed, aperture, location and date.

You could record your observations and insights about the formal elements and visual characteristics of other artists' works that you have observed through your research into contextual sources. For example:

- You might use image processing software to give one of your own images the colours, textures or surface qualities of a secondary source image (see Figures 3.45 and 3.50).
- You could record insights into visual and design characteristics such as composition, balance, harmony and aesthetics by producing sketches, studies or finished pieces which show that you have addressed these in your work; see Case studies 30 and 33 on Photography and Fine Art.

3.50 *Recording stages of development*

> **Remember**
>
> Record observations, insights and intentions in the ways in which your ideas and intentions have developed.

- You could record how your ideas and intentions are directly related to a major style, movement or the approaches that another artist or designer has taken. In the following Case study, number 32, for example, links to Pop Art and Rauschenberg are made.

Case study 32

Recording insights in Graphic Communication

Acheson uses drawings, photographs and colour studies to record his insights into Pop Art and Rauschenberg's working methods. These studies are supported by insights which communicate Acheson's critical understanding, as well as his ideas and plans for his work in the period of supervised time (Figure 3.51).

AQA Examiner's tip

Record how your own work links to your contextual sources.

3.51 *Working drawing for final layout*

3.52 *Acheson's final piece*

Case study 33

Recording insights in Fine Art

As Lisa developed her ideas towards the final composition, she recorded her insights into how different techniques and media can be used to create particular effects. Her use of a varied pencil line and tone to suggest form, and the exploration of texture using monochrome, demonstrate an understanding of the principles of Cubism. Her intentions are recorded in some double page layouts which have selected areas treated in paint in order to refine her handling of colour (Figure 3.53).

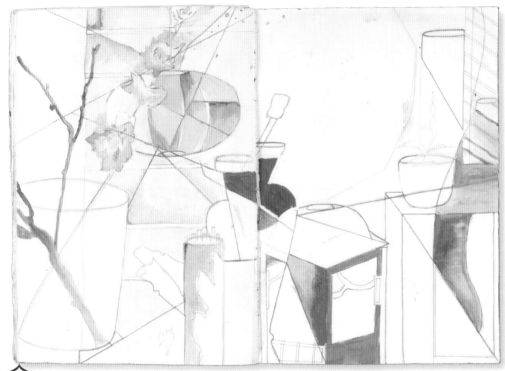

3.53 *Composition layout*

Lisa's sketchbook shows:

- the recording of ideas and insights in both visual and written form
- clear and focused visual recording from both first-hand and secondary sources
- recording the development of ideas and intentions
- drawings in a range of media which are used to record formal elements such as line, tone and form
- recording of understanding and insights which inform the development of the final painting.

3.54 *Braque* Clarinet and Bottle of Rum on Mantlepiece *(1911)*

3.55 *Final still life painting*

Reflecting on your work and progress

The ways in which you use media, materials, processes and techniques, and develop skills can all be used to provide evidence of your intentions and your understanding of Art and Design. You should also reflect on your work by:

- looking back and considering what and how you have recorded
- thinking about how you have selected and developed your ideas and images using various media and processes
- considering ways in which you have used contextual material to inform the development of your work
- thinking about how your work responds to the starting point or brief
- considering ways in which you could develop your ideas further.

A record of the reflection process could include:

- studies based on the work of artists and designers which record your observations about particular aspects of their work such as use of colour, layout, construction, form, working methods or techniques

- your observations and insights in analytical sketches, diagrams or annotated illustrations
- development studies which record ideas and variations on a design, image or construction
- work that records developments in your ideas.

The case studies in this chapter show different ways of recording ideas, observations and insights.

3.56 *Eileen Agar* Angel of Anarchy *(second version) (1940)*

Case study 34

Recording intentions in Graphic Communication

Acheson presented a series of cropped and trimmed photographs which he analysed in order to identify the characteristics and features of his contextual

3.57 *Sketchbook study recording possible idea*

kerboodle!

3.58 *Rauschenberg* Reservoir (1961)

3.59 *Studies recording developing intentions*

3.60 *Peter Blake* Toy Shop (1962)

sources. These images led to further exploratory studies in which he recorded his intentions (see Figure 3.57).

In a study sheet on Rauschenberg (Figure 3.59), Acheson recorded his insights into the ways in which th e artist developed a response to his contemporary culture, and the ways in which different media, text and image make his work unique.

Acheson records the possibilities of using complex layers of readily observed patterns, designs and letter forms to create the feeling of a particular era.

See Figure 3.60 for Peter Blake's approach to recording by using memorabilia in his *Toy Shop* (1962).

Learning outcomes

Having read this chapter you should now be able to:

record in visual and other forms your ideas, observations and insights

select and record from sources appropriate to your chosen theme, starting point or brief

record in sketchbooks, journals, logs or on mounted sheets

record your insights and intentions

use digital media for recording observations and ideas.

A personal, informed and meaningful response in realising your intentions should develop through the process of your work, in the way that you respond to your **source material** and develop your ideas.

You should realise your intentions in a personal, informed and meaningful way, not only in the presentation of ideas, a final piece or a series of related works, but also across a project as a whole. Your response should demonstrate critical understanding and make connections between different elements of your work.

A personal response

Your response should be personal in the way that you select a starting point, a theme or a brief, in the way that you identify and generate ideas, and select appropriate source materials to work from. You will choose a starting point that interests you and work from you own personal experience of the source material you have selected. A personal response is the way that you interpret and respond to ideas and your source material. It is personal to you because the realisation of your intentions comes from your own personal investigation, and you are expressing or communicating your own ideas and reactions to what you have seen and experienced. We each see things differently and use our imagination and understanding in different ways.

An informed response

Investigation of your chosen source material, contextual material and your experiments with materials, media, processes and techniques will inform the development of your personal response. It will be informed by previous experience, by the understanding that you have developed in previous projects, and it might also be informed by other sources, things that you have seen, read or listened to.

The development of a personal response can be informed by:

- investigating ideas and your source materials
- investigating the work of others
- investigating contextual material and other sources
- experimenting with and developing your understanding of media, processes and techniques
- developing your analytical and observational skills
- developing your understanding of visual elements such as line, tone, form, space, colour and composition.

Investigating appropriate works by other artists, craftspeople and designers can help you to develop an informed personal response to ideas, source materials and media and techniques.

∞ links

See Chapter 1 for more about using contextual materials and investigation.

See Chapter 2 for more about experimenting with media, processes and techniques, and developing skills.

See Chapter 3 for more about recording observations and insights.

A meaningful response

Your response should be meaningful in the way that it develops from your investigations and in the ways that your ideas have meaning. Develop clear intentions in the investigation and development of your work, and in making a personal and meaningful response to your chosen starting point. If your work has a sense of purpose and a sense of direction, it is more likely that your response will have meaning. Thinking seriously about your work and the choices and decisions you make in its development will help you to respond in a meaningful way in realising your intentions. Engaging with your work, getting involved, will help to make it more meaningful.

Be inquisitive and ask questions through your work. You might, for example, be exploring a natural object and, through your response to it, asking questions about its appearance, its qualities and characteristics. In other words, you might be exploring and discovering things about its shape, form, structure, colour and texture.

The bars on the bus window and kitchen window draw attention to the barrier between outside and inside.

OWN PHOTOS

Walker Evans→

Every day activities, window a line between interior and exterior

Robert Frank

4.2 *Looking out – a sketchbook page*

An artist's personal response in Fine Art

Ian Murphy is a professional artist based in the north west of England whose drawings and paintings are personal responses to the many journeys he has undertaken. Landscape and historical architecture are the main subjects of his work.

'The most important images I produce are contained within my sketchbooks. These are the catalysts for all the exciting developments within the studio environment. The majority of the drawings are black and white, mainly using graphite, rubbers and fine-line pens. I try to draw quickly, ensuring that the main focus to the study is the right composition but with a fluid, expressive use of marks.'

Ian's drawings, responses from his fieldwork, are developed in the studio. In his 'Venice' series, Ian made several visits to the Italian city to study architectural

IMPOSING & MONUMENTAL
CORNERSTONE
FORBIDDEN CITY

SWEEPING CURVE AT THE
CORNER OF THE ROOF
LEADS YOUR EYE FROM THE
FOREGROUND STRUCTURE THROUGH
TO THE PEAK OF THE ROOF AND
THE DRAGON

kerboodle!

4.4 *Architectural detail, Manchester*

4.5 *Architectural detail*

features between developing the series of drawings in his studio. Ian's intentions are clear: to respond in an informed and meaningful way to the atmosphere and character of his subject, the crumbling facades of ancient Venetian buildings. His response is personal, meaningful and informed by his investigations of his source material. Experimentation with media and techniques, and the way that Ian develops his ideas, also contribute to the development of his personal response in realising his intentions.

4.6 Three Kings in the Chasm, *Large graphite drawing – Venice*

4.7 'Scars of Life 1', *Large drawing – Macau*

⬭⬭links

Find out about Ian Murphy at
www.ianmurphyartist.com

■ Developing a personal visual language

The case studies in this book and in the online resource connected with it illustrate the ways in which artists and students have each developed their own personal language in responding in an informed and meaningful way to ideas, issues, themes or briefs. A personal visual language is not something that you can suddenly switch on.

In making a response that is personal, the way that you see and understand things can change and develop as your work progresses. The qualities and characteristics of your work can alter as you respond to different ideas and source material, and as you respond to different materials, media, processes and techniques. You might, for example, respond in different ways in different projects. You might respond in different ways in one project. In response to a particular starting point, different students might respond in an analytical way or an expressive way, but each will develop a **visual language** that is distinctly personal in its response, in the way that it communicates ideas and realises intentions.

Key terms

Visual language: the ways that we use visual elements such as line, tone, colour and form, in a personal way.

Case study 36

Developing a personal response in Fine Art

Katharine responded in a personal way to the theme of 'Everyday life'. Her personal involvement in her work is demonstrated in her own photographs on which she based her investigation and in the realisation of her intentions in two paintings. Drawing from a selection of these images, investigating the ways other artists have composed figures in different locations, experimenting with different media and techniques all informed the development of Katharine's response.

4.9 *Monochrome study*

Mondrian

Blocks of colour
representing shape
and form, straight lines
in Mondrian's work give
a straight interior
feel like the window
in Vermeer's work

Vermeer links
the exterior and
interior spaces
with the open
window.
Vermeer uses
his paintings
to tell stories,
the woman
holds a letter
from a loved
one.

Vermeer.

4.10 *Developing a personal response*

■ Critical understanding

Critical understanding is about making appropriate and informed choices, connections and decisions in your work. The decisions you make in developing an idea and selecting appropriate resources and materials will be informed by the understanding, knowledge and experience gained from your previous work and by the understanding that you are developing in the work that you are doing now. It is about developing opinions and preferences in the ways that you choose and respond to ideas, selecting appropriate source materials and in the ways that you investigate and develop your own ideas. It is also about the way in which you make decisions in directing your work and the way that discoveries you make in one study lead to another and to the realisation of your intentions.

Responding critically to briefs, ideas, themes or issues

In choosing an idea, theme or issue to investigate and to develop your work from, you will use critical understanding in making an informed decision and judgement in selecting one starting point over another.

∞ links

See Chapter 3 for more about recording ideas, observations and insights.

See Chapter 1 for more about developing ideas.

4.11 *A design sheet analysing a brief*

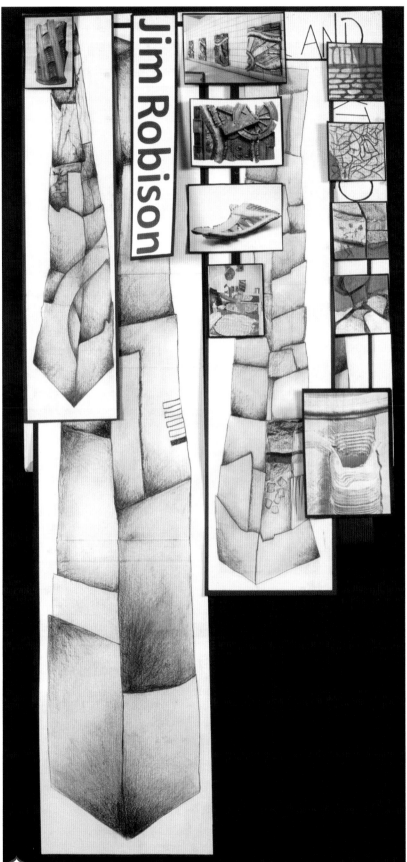

4.12 *Large scale design sheet*

You will have preferences that are informed by your interests, your experiences as a person, and your knowledge and understanding of art and design from previous work. Your preferences might be informed by:

- your understanding of the work of other artists, craftspeople and designers
- your understanding of the art and artefacts of other cultures and different times
- your understanding of materials, techniques and processes
- other sources such as material that you have read or heard.

In your investigation of a starting point and developing a personal response to an idea, theme or issue, you will respond critically in developing a focus to your investigation and to the development of your work. You might, for example, identify and choose a particular slant or angle in your interpretation of an issue. In responding to a landscape you might choose to focus on light and the weather, on texture and surface or on the land-form itself. In making these sorts of choices, you will demonstrate critical understanding.

If you are responding to a brief, you will respond critically by making decisions about different ways in which the brief's requirements can be met. You will consider and analyse what is required, the limitations and constraints that the requirements impose on you, as well as the

Remember

You can demonstrate critical understanding entirely through your practical work.

AQA **Examiner's tip**

Provide evidence of critical understanding in your practical work.

links

See Chapter 1 for more ideas about using contextual material.

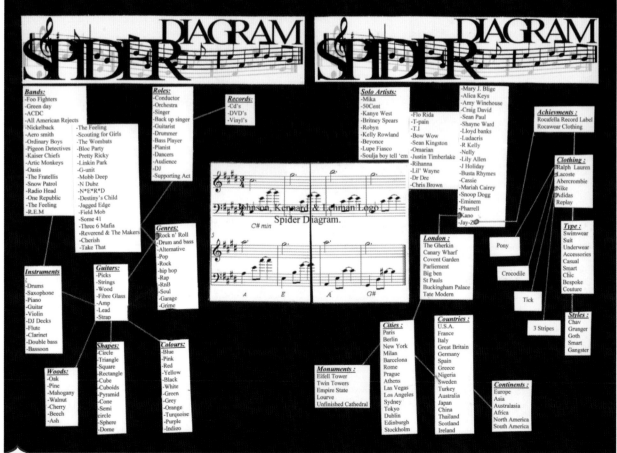

4.13 *A mind map for a design project*

opportunities the brief presents you to develop a personal, informed and meaningful response.

You should also use critical understanding in responding to the ideas, issues and themes in the work of other artists, craftspeople and designers. You might investigate the ways that a particular artist or several artists have responded to a social issue, a subject, a theme or an idea, or the way a designer has developed a response to a design brief. Critical understanding will be needed in choosing works that are appropriate to your own intentions and in understanding their meaning and purpose.

Case study 37

An artist demonstrating critical understanding in Fine Art

In each series of his paintings, Ian Murphy demonstrates critical understanding in the development of his response. He considers a number of locations, looking at character, atmosphere and their potential as material for his work. Ian demonstrates critical understanding in expressing his preference for a particular idea or location and in the ways that he decides to work from one location rather than another.

Ian responds to the natural environment, to the time of day and the sense of time having passed. He says that his drawings and paintings are often a personal response to the 'landscape's amazing structure and power' and he chooses 'dramatic and inhospitable places' to work from. Ian's atmospheric

4.14 Tranquility, *Oil paint and mixed media on canvas, showing Chinese roof structure*

works reflect a sense of mystery and wonder about the landscape, and his response is both personal and meaningful. In choosing particular aspects of the landscape to investigate and to respond to, and in the choices and decisions that he makes in his work, Ian demonstrates critical understanding.

Demonstrating critical understanding

You can demonstrate critical understanding in making informed choices, decisions and connections in your work and in developing your own opinions and preferences.

You should:

- make informed decisions in selecting an appropriate starting point, demonstrating critical understanding in choosing one idea rather than another
- demonstrate understanding of your chosen idea, theme, issue or brief
- make informed choices and decisions in the investigation and development of your ideas, in experimenting with media and in realising your intentions
- demonstrate your understanding of formal elements in your own work and in the work of others
- develop informed opinions and preferences of your own
- demonstrate critical understanding in the way that one study leads to another
- make connections between one image and another
- make connections between different elements of your work.

You should demonstrate critical understanding in ways that are appropriate to your intentions and there are different ways of doing this. You could provide evidence of critical understanding in the way that your preparatory work reflects the choices and decisions you make as the work progresses. Presenting one image alongside another can make clear the connection you have made between them, the way a work by another artist or designer has informed the development of your own work, or the way that one of your studies has led to another. A sequence of studies, samples or images, can show the way that you have explored alternatives and made decisions about the direction of your work in developing ideas and in realising your intentions. For example, you might demonstrate critical understanding in a series of compositional or design ideas, in making an analytical study looking at the handling of tone in a work by an artist, or in the way that you have selected a medium and technique for a working drawing, a design or a final piece.

Where it is appropriate, you might choose to support your work with evidence of critical understanding presented in other forms, which might include writing or speaking. You might, for example, annotate images with brief notes or bullet points in which you analyse a work by another artist, craftsperson or designer. You might decide to note the meaning, purpose and context of an artefact where, perhaps, a different tradition, custom and belief are important to your understanding of the work. You might think that in some aspect of your work your studies do

⊂⊃links

See Chapter 3 for more ideas about recording.

Remember

You might choose to provide evidence of critical understanding in other forms, which might include writing or speaking.

not make clear the choices, decisions and connections you have made, and choose to support your practical work with annotations. These should have a critical element and make clear the reasons why you have chosen to develop your work in a particular way.

Case study 38

Demonstrating critical understanding in Three-Dimensional Design

In this Unit 2 Externally Set Task, Jake responded in ceramics to the theme of 'Decoration'. He explored impressed and applied surface texture and pattern by using similar techniques to those used in the sculptural ceramics by artist Jim Robison. Having investigated the sculpturesque towers of Antoni Gaudi's *Sagrada Familia*, Jake developed a personal response to the theme and realised his intentions in the form of a ceramic tower. Jake's work demonstrates critical understanding in the ways that he has formed opinions and shown preferences in developing his work and in realising his intentions, and also in the ways that he has made decisions in working towards a conclusion and made connections between different aspects of his work.

4.15 *Jim Robison working on* Rufford Vase

4.16 *Jim Robison* Rufford Vase

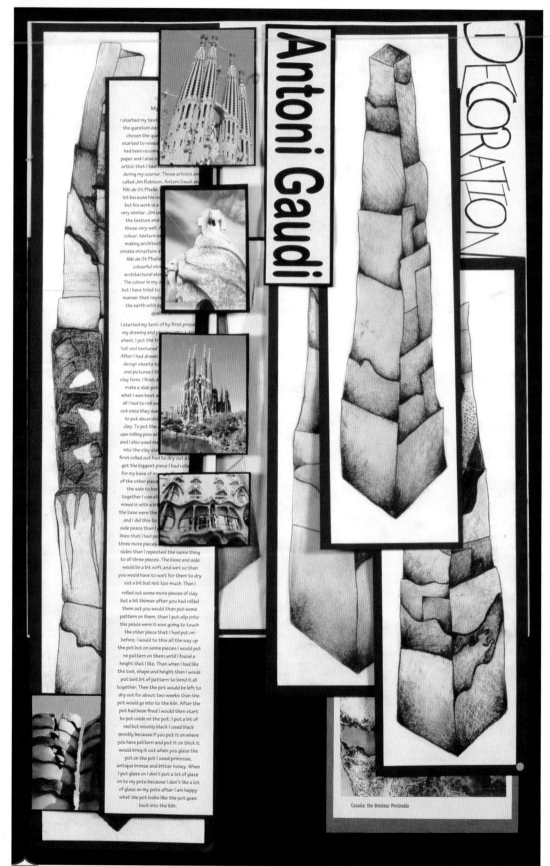

4.17 *One of Jake's design sheets*

4.18 *Decorated vessel by Jake*

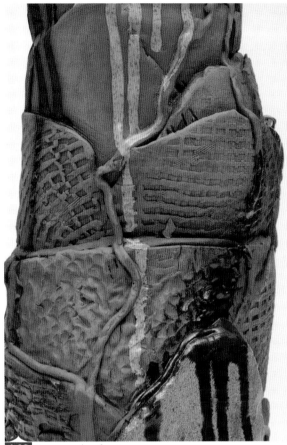

4.19 *Impressed surfaces*

4.20 *Antoni Gaudi* La Sagrada Familia

AQA **Examiner's tip**

If you choose to present your work in a sketchbook, use it like a diary by recording ideas and developments as they happen.

Responding critically to ideas in Fine Art

Katharine has responded in a personal way to the theme 'Interiors'. She investigated contextual material which included Johannes Vermeer, Edward Hopper, Walker Evans, Robert Frank and Cindy Sherman to help develop her understanding of how different artists have composed images from the interior environment. She has demonstrated critical understanding in selecting appropriate examples, in responding critically by making studies from them and in presenting personal opinion in brief annotations.

Katharine's critical understanding is shown also in the ways she has expressed her preferences through her choice of source material and in the way that she has chosen a particular idea in developing her response and in realising her intentions. She chose to explore light and atmosphere in the paintings of Vermeer and Hopper. Katharine also developed alternative compositions and looked critically at her own work in choosing the direction for her final outcome. Critical understanding is evident in the ways that she has made decisions in developing her response, in the way that she has related one study to another and has made connections between the different elements of her work.

⊂⊃ links

Find out about Edward Hopper at **www.artchive.com**

Find out about Cindy Sherman at **www.cindysherman.com**

Find out about Robert Frank at **www.tate.org.uk**

Find out about Johannes Vermeer at **www.essentialvermeer.com**

Find out about Walker Evans at **www.biographybase.com/ biography/Evans_Walker**

I used ink, and black and white paint to give an expressive, alive feeling to the pictures, along with continuing to explore interior space.

4.21 *Monochrome studies*

→ The window allows the closed interior of the *Kusto* have a feeling of space through the vast expanse of sea and sky beyond.

Exploring everyday life experiences in interior spaces. Windows hold a connection between the space of the outside world and a closed in space.

Hopper

4.22 *Sketchbook pages*

Walker Evans

The bars on the bus window and kitchen window draw attention to the barrier between outside and inside.

Everyday activities, window a line between interior and exterior.

Robert Frank

4.23 *Studies of interiors*

kerboodle!

4.24 *Johannes Vermeer (1658–1660)* The Milkmaid

4.25 *Edward Hopper* Compartment C, Car 293 (1938)

Case study 40

Responding critically to ideas in Graphic Communication

Daniel has responded to a Graphic Communication brief to design a **logo** for Johnson, Kennard and Lehman, a company that makes and sells musical instruments.

The personal nature of his work is reflected in the ways that he has demonstrated critical understanding by developing preferences and opinions in choosing his ideas, in selecting appropriate source materials and in realising his intentions in a personal, informed and meaningful way. Daniel demonstrated his preferences and critical understanding in selecting appropriate contextual material that includes works by Juan Gris and examples of graphic design. In the investigation and his response, he has made connections between images and between different aspects of his work, responding critically to source material, compositional alternatives and ideas, and in using the formal elements of line, colour and surface appropriately.

In developing his personal response, Daniel analysed his digital images and responded critically to them through further image manipulation. In responding to the brief, Daniel considered different ideas in which he has demonstrated an understanding of the brief's requirements and his personal preferences in the presentation of alternative design proposals. Critical understanding is evident too, in the ways that Daniel has made appropriate connections between different elements of his work in realising his intentions.

Key terms

Logo: a logo is a distinctive sign or symbol that identifies a product, company or agency.

∞ links

See Chapter 1 for more about using contextual material.

See Chapter 2 for more about using materials, techniques and processes to refine ideas.

4.26 *Instrument designs*

kerboodle!

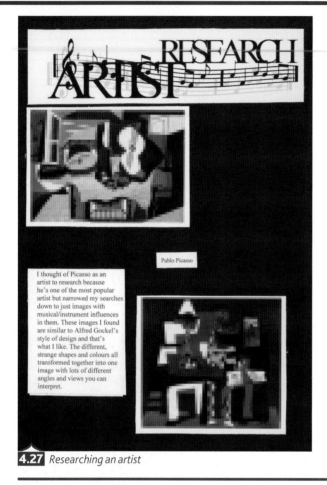

4.27 *Researching an artist*

4.28 *Looking at contextual sources*

Case study 41

Responding critically to ideas in Applied Art

Jessica has responded to a Unit 2 Externally Set Task that required design work which included opportunities for the design of a poster, CD cover, a brochure or museum banner to promote a touring exhibition with a maritime theme, entitled 'Sea, stars and time'.

Jessica has chosen to investigate and develop her ideas for a cover design for a CD. She visited a regional maritime museum where she made drawings and took photographs of appropriate source material. Jessica took the opportunity to speak to museum staff to gain knowledge of the maritime theme and, through interview and conversation, she investigated the possibilities that would serve the client. She responded critically to the requirements of the brief by considering different possibilities for her investigation. Her practical work, supported by annotation, demonstrates her critical response to ideas. Her investigations of designs for CD covers and the work of artist Robert Rauschenberg, also demonstrate a critical response in the ways that she chose particular examples and made connections with them in realising her intentions and developing a personal response.

In exploring alternative compositions and surface effects, Jessica has responded critically to ideas and demonstrated critical understanding in her

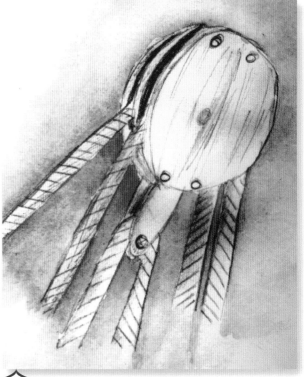

4.30 *Drawing from source material*

4.29 *Observations from the maritime museum, putting the work into a context*

preferences, opinions and decisions. She has chosen to present her work in a sequence that makes connections between images and has enabled her to make a critical evaluation of her work. Jessica has responded critically to ideas in relation to the requirements and constraints of the brief.

4.31 *Robert Rauschenberg* Tracer (1963)

4.32 *Responding critically to an artist's work*

Realising intentions

You can realise your intentions in bringing an investigation towards some form of resolution and conclusion in a personal outcome in response to your starting point. Realisation can take various forms and may have a single or several related outcomes. Your intention might be to produce a single, final or conclusive piece of work or a series of related works. In Applied Art, the requirements may be more specific, if you are responding to a brief that requires a particular outcome.

Where appropriate, you could realise your intentions in work of a developmental nature, for example, in the form of maquettes or design ideas. If you are a Textile Design student, you might design and make a wall-hanging or realise your intentions in a series of related **samplers**. In Three-Dimensional Design, you might realise your intentions in a fully resolved, finished, ceramic sculpture or produce a series of models or maquettes of a developmental nature which are appropriate to your intentions. In Photography, you might realise your intentions in a single image, or a series of related images.

You might also realise your intentions at different stages of the work, in the form of an analytical drawing, a working drawing, a sheet of design ideas, a maquette or model, an exploration of stitching techniques, or a sequence of photographs that is the end to a particular line of investigation. Realisations such as these could mark a point in the journey of your investigation and the development of your ideas.

The Externally Set Task, Unit 2, requires you to make a personal response to one of the starting points on the examination paper and to conclude this reponse in a period of supervised time.

AQA **Examiner's tip**

In Applied Art, take account of the specific requirements of the brief.

Key terms

Sampler: in Textile Design, a small working study that shows what a finished constructed or printed textile will look like.

Design sheet: a sheet of studies that demonstrates or presents the development of an idea, sometimes in a logical sequence or progression of images, sometimes showing the exploration of alternative ideas.

Mood board: usually in the form of collage, photo-montage or collected materials, the mood-board is often used in textiles and interior design to explore initial ideas about colour, tone and texture.

In the period of supervised time you might:

- create a completely finished practical outcome such as a painting, a print, a sculpture or a design
- produce a series of related works, maquettes or models of a developmental nature.

AQA **Examiner's tip**

You must bring your own work to a conclusion in a personal, practical outcome.

Case study 42

Realising intentions in Applied Art in response to an Externally Set Task

Jessica has presented a personal response to an Externally Set Task starting point in which she has realised her intentions in the form of a packaging design for a CD. Responding to a brief in Unit 2 requires focused planning and clear intentions, as you are working within a set period of time, as well as responding to the specific demands of the client brief.

Jessica's artwork makes use of transparency and layering in a multi-image composition. She has chosen to support her practical work with notes, **design sheets** and **mood boards**. Each of the composite images on the front, outside and inner sleeve of the CD packaging include different information relevant to the brief. The final design proposal has been (continued on page 150)

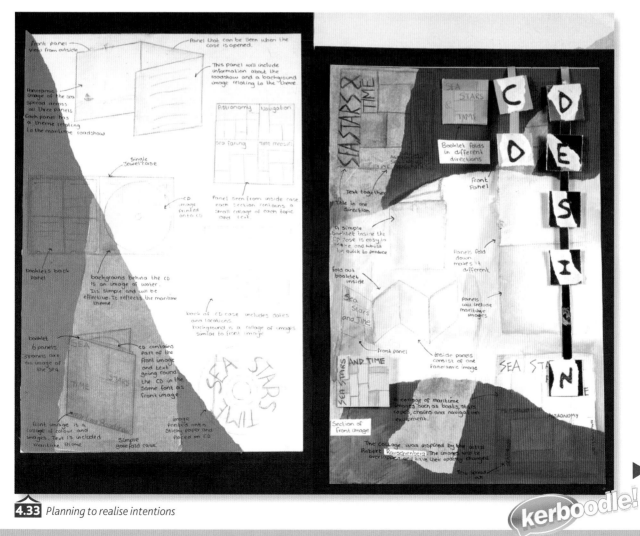

4.33 *Planning to realise intentions*

4.34 *Starting to develop ideas in Photoshop*

4.35 *Realising intentions*

4.36 *CD cover design*

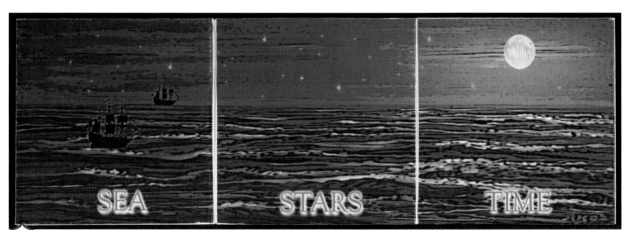

4.37 *The folded panels with image*

completed with a printed CD disc and this preferred proposal has been supported by a number of alternative designs for the client to choose from. Jessica has realised her intentions in different ways, in her final design proposal, in alternative designs and through the personal, visual language she has developed in her response to the starting point.

4.38 *The folded panels with information*

Case study 43

Realising intentions in Three-Dimensional Design

4.39 *Decorated vessel by Jake*

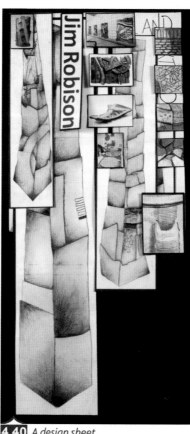

4.40 *A design sheet*

Jake realised his intentions in a **ceramic** construction, in the form of a tower, constructed as a slab vessel made in sections of terracotta clay. The clay panels are detailed with impressed textures and patterns and further embellished with cut and extruded attachments. Following **biscuit firing** the ceramic vessel was treated with red iron oxide and a partial **glaze**.

His outcome is supported by two large design sheets which provide evidence of the development of his personal response to the starting point. His intentions have been realised in three-dimensional work and graphic illustration. Supported with written material, Jake has made connections between these different elements of his work.

Did you know ??????

Clay surfaces can be pierced with materials such as metal, wire, and nails before being fired, and coloured glass fragments can be melted into the fired clay to embed glazed detail. Ceramics can be a very experimental area of practice.

Realising intentions using digital media

Digital and **electronic media** are used extensively in all areas of art and design to record observations, to resource and develop ideas, to experiment with, explore and manipulate images. Particularly in Graphic Communication and Photography, but also in Fine Art and Three-Dimensional Design, these media can be used to realise intentions.

In Three-Dimensional Design, computer software programs can be used to visualise how an installation or construction might relate to a specific site such as a shopping centre, a cultural centre or another public space. In Textile Design, digital media might be used to demonstrate how a garment looks on a model or to visualise how a

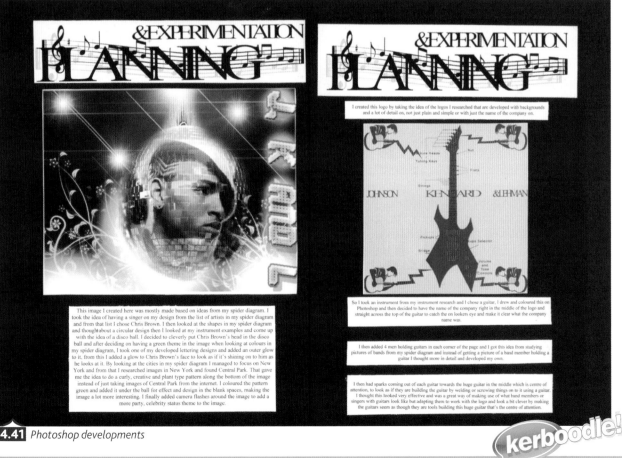

4.41 *Photoshop developments*

kerboodle!

constructed textile, wall hanging or tapestry might look on a large scale in a public location. In Graphic Communication, illustration, designs for print, packaging, company logos and promotional materials can all be produced using computer software, scanners, printers and digital media such as the digital camera. Realisations such as poster designs, illustrated pages, book covers, labelling and packaging designs can be produced and presented using electronic media.

In Photography, you might realise your intentions using light-based media in the form of digital cameras, video cameras and camcorders. Images can be manipulated using computer software, and in Photography, Fine Art and Graphic Communication, moving images can be combined with sound. For example, an animation for a TV channel or a website might include sound.

In Fine Art, images, surfaces, textures, and colour can be manipulated, overlapped and built up in layers to produce realisations in the form of abstractions or photo-montage. Digital photography, moving images, light and sound can also be used to produce realisations in a Fine Art context.

Alternative approaches

Other possible ways to realise intentions include:

- combinations of photographic, sculptural and graphic elements
- creating an installation work for a specific site
- combining sound and image
- combining traditional and digital media
- animation, motion graphics, film or video
- temporary, ephemeral, fragile work that needs to be documented before it decays or disappears.

⬯links

See Chapters 1, 2 and 3 for more ideas about using digital and electronic media.

Presenting a personal response using digital and electronic media

In Graphic Communication, you can use digital and electronic media to make a personal response by manipulating images, **typography**, composition and layouts. In Photography, you can develop a personal response through the creative use of the camera and by using software such as Adobe Photoshop. In Textile Design, you might use digital media to make a personal response through manipulating pattern, texture and colour, presenting alternative colour schemes and visuals. In Three-Dimensional Design, you might use software to model environments and to show the three-dimensional appearance of sculptures and vessels. Surface designs can be experimented with and explored before being applied onto a three-dimensional form.

Digital media are valuable resources that can be used for making a response in different ways:

- recording ideas
- developing ideas in a personal way
- documenting work in progress

- investigating contextual material
- realising intentions
- presenting artwork.

You can present a personal response and realise your intentions using digital media in different ways.

You might:

- make a video or film using digital effects
- create a series of related images
- present your response in the form of a journal of digital images
- present a short animated sequence
- combine digital artwork with traditional materials
- create a digital image to be printed on different surfaces.

Jessica, studying Applied Art, and Daniel, studying Graphic Communication, each made use of digital photography and computer software programs in developing their work in a personal way. Jessica used electronic media to compose the different elements of her work into a personal response to her brief. Daniel used computer software as an appropriate medium to develop his personal response and to realise his intentions in designing a company logo.

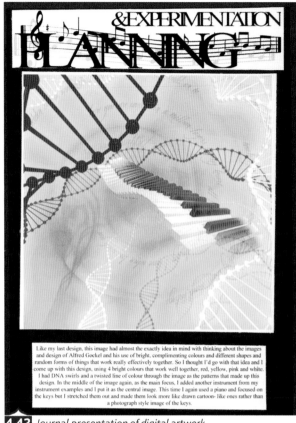

4.42 *Journal presentation of digital artwork*

Making connections between different elements of your work

Making connections between different elements of your work is important in the investigation and development of your ideas, in making a personal response and in realising your intentions. As well as visual elements, your work might include written, oral or other elements, such as sound or performance.

Critical understanding, the way that you can develop and form opinions and have preferences, your ability to analyse, evaluate and make comparisons and the way that you can make informed decisions, should enable you to make visual links and connections between different stages and between different elements of your work.

Making connections between elements of your work describes the way in which a project is a journey in which each part of the process of investigation, experimentation, recording, developing ideas, making a personal response and realising intentions, fits together, with each part of the process informing the others.

You might make connections between the development of your own work and material through:

- reading, such as in books, plays, newspapers or on the internet
- hearing, such as performances of music, environmental sound in the natural or man-made world, or in speeches, interviews or debates on radio or TV
- seeing or taking part in events, such as concerts, dance performances, festivals or other events.

> **Remember**
>
> You can use digital and electronic media in different ways to present your response and to realise your intentions.

You might make connections between the development and realisation of your work, and work you have produced in a workshop or in association with another artist, or the observations you have made from works seen on a gallery visit.

Written work in the form of notes or annotated images can sometimes make clear the connections between different elements of your work. For example, you might make clearer the connections you have made between contextual material and the development of your own ideas. Where elements of the journey of your work are not obvious in a purely visual way, you might provide helpful insights in written or in other forms.

You can also make connections between different aspects of your work orally, in discussion with a group of other students, or with your art teacher. You might have the opportunity to give a PowerPoint presentation or use sound and video to give a presentation or an interview in which you explain the connections between various elements of your work.

Presentation

In Assessment Objective 4 you should present a personal response in which you demonstrate critical understanding, realise your intentions and make connections between visual and other elements of your work. Art and Design is a visual subject and the quality of your presentation is important. Good work can be spoilt by poor presentation and organisation, untidy writing, over-elaborate or unnecessary lettering or labelling. In the way that you present your work, aim to make clear the journey of your investigation and the development of your ideas.

Case study 44

Presenting a personal response in Fine Art

Katharine has responded in a personal way to the theme of 'Interiors'.

In her sketchbook, Katharine investigated several lines of enquiry in making a personal response to the theme. She explored different types of interiors which included the interior of a bus and a domestic interior. Informed by her investigation of the work of artists that included Vermeer, Hopper and Cindy Sherman, she responded to the idea of the figure in an enclosed space.

In presenting her work, Katharine made a meaningful response in making connections between different elements of her work. Her investigation, experimentation, recording and the development of her ideas, connect with and inform each other. In presenting her preparatory work, she made meaningful connections between images that are appropriate to her intentions and these demonstrate the way in which she has developed her ideas and her personal response to the theme (Figures 4.43–4.46).

Katharine realised her intentions in a sketchbook and two related paintings, acrylic on canvas, each approximately 90 x 60 cm (Figures 4.44–4.46).

4.43 *On the bus*

OWN PICTURES.

4.44 *Informing a personal response*

kerboodle!

4.45 *Figure in a room – monochrome study*

4.46 *Figure in a Room*

Work can be presented in various ways, in the form of mounted sheets of studies, sketchbooks, design sheets, workbooks, journals, files or well-organised folders. You might make use of electronic media to present your work on CD, as an electronic sketchbook, a video, an animation, or as a PowerPoint presentation. You might use sound, light or present your work in the form of an installation.

Case study 45

Presenting a response in Graphic Communication

Daniel responded to a brief that required the design of a logo for a company that makes and sells musical instruments.

In realising his intentions, Daniel has presented a personal, informed and meaningful response to his chosen starting point and to his source materials. He presented his work in an A4 file which documents and provides evidence of his investigation of several ideas and his design proposals (Figures 4.47–4.49).

Daniel's work is presented in sequence and his mounted images are supported by appropriate and meaningful annotations which add to our understanding of his response. Daniel has offered the client a range of different design ideas alongside his own preferred design proposal, his main outcome, which is presented on a larger scale (Figure 4.50).

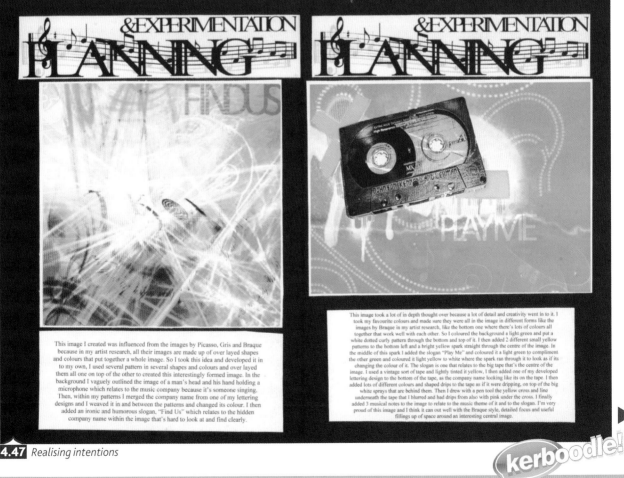

This image I created was influenced from the images by Picasso, Gris and Braque because in my artist research, all their images are made up of over layed shapes and colours that put together a whole image. So I took this idea and developed it in to my own, I used several pattern in several shapes and colours and over layed them all on top of the other to created this interestingly formed image. In the background I vaguely outlined the image of a man's head and his hand holding a microphone which relates to the music company because it's someone singing. Then, within my patterns I merged the company name from one of my lettering designs and I weaved it in and between the patterns and changed its colour. I then added an ironic and humorous slogan, "Find Us" which relates to the hidden company name within the image that's hard to look at and find clearly.

This image took a lot of in depth thought over because a lot of detail and creativity went in to it. I took my favourite colours and made sure they were all in the image in different forms like the images by Braque in my artist research, like the bottom one where there's lots of colours all together that work well with each other. So I coloured the background a light green and put a white dotted curly pattern through the bottom and top of it. I then added 2 different small yellow patterns to the bottom left and a bright yellow spark straight through the centre of the image. In the middle of this spark I added the slogan "Play Me" and coloured it a light green to compliment the other green and coloured it light yellow to white where the spark ran through it to look as if its changing the colour of it. The slogan is one that relates to the big tape that's the centre of the image. I used a vintage sort of tape and lightly tinted it yellow, I then added one of my developed lettering design to the bottom of the tape, as the company name looking like its on the tape. I then added lots of different colours and shaped drips to the tape as if it were dripping, on top of the big white sprays that are behind them. Then I drew with a pen tool the yellow cross and line underneath the tape that I blurred and had drips from also with pink under the cross. I finally added 3 musical notes to the image to relate to the music theme of it and to the slogan. I'm very proud of this image and I think it can out well with the Braque style, detailed focus and useful fillings up of space around an interesting central image.

4.47 *Realising intentions*

kerboodle!

I took one of my favourite female artists from the list of artists in my spider diagram, which was Rihanna and I decided to draw my own image of here instead of just taking one from the internet. I started off like this, creating a shaded and toned image of her face with eyes and eyebrows.

&EXPERIMENTATION PLANNING

&EXPERIMENTATION PLANNING

I then edited an image of her I researched and I put the image I drew over the edited one I made to create this very interesting and detailed image of her face and I think its really effective, adding the edited colour of her complexion with the toned and shaded one I created and her eyes I drew with her real lips and nose, it creates an overall out of the ordinary image.

STOP/EJECT

I took this image I made and I used the same technique to draw my own saxophone instead of just sticking one on the image that didn't have my own personal creativity on it. I put this saxophone in front of the Rihanna image and I then got the idea of musical notes from an image I researched in my artist research by Digital Music Art and added my own pattern of musical notes coming out of the end of the saxophone as if it's playing music. I then took one of my lettering designs and developed it which again added my own personal touch on because I developed an internet lettering design. I changed the colour to match the picture and finally, I studied the idea of CD's and DVD's in my spider diagram and come up with the buttons that are on CD and DVD players. I then added 3 buttons that are highly recognisable as there on every CD player and this relates to music highly and everyone knows what they are so I added them underneath the saxophone and changed their colours to compliment the rest of the image.

4.48 *Design ideas*

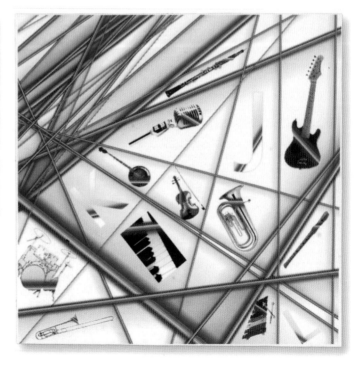

4.49 *Alternative designs*

4.50 *Daniel's final design proposal*

Take care in organising and presenting the layout of your studies or images on mounts, or on pages in sketchbooks, workbooks or files. Demonstrate your critical understanding in considering how one image relates to another and by grouping together studies and images in a meaningful way. You might, for example, want to show some of your work in a particular sequence. Balance the size and scale of your studies, also monochrome and colour, so that one image does not dominate another, and think about the weight of images on a sheet or page. Ask yourself if a layout looks top-heavy or unbalanced. The size of individual studies will often determine what goes where and it is a good idea to try different layouts before you glue them into position.

Work can be presented in different ways:

- sketchbooks, design sheets or mounted sheets
- journals or workbooks
- CD-Roms or PowerPoint presentations

Remember

- Your work can be spoilt by poor presentation.
- If you are mounting work, try different layouts.

AQA Examiner's tip

- Group studies and images together in a meaningful way.
- Present your work in an appropriate way.

- video or film
- models or maquettes
- a well-organised folder.

You might decide to make a spoken presentation to explain and support your work. This could be documented and presented as a sound recording or video.

Presenting three-dimensional work

The presentation of your personal response might be in the form of sculpture, maquettes for sculptures, architectural models, stage set designs, packaging or fashion **mock-ups**, pots, tiles or test pieces. In presenting work in sculpture, ceramics or installations, you might photograph the work in progress and the final outcome against a suitable background. Lighting might be especially important in the presentation of three-dimensional work. Photographing a construction with carefully manipulated lighting might support your work by showing your intentions more clearly. Fashion items can be photographed to demonstrate the work displayed on a model. Work that includes architectural models, sculpture or three-dimensional constructions might be supported by photographs, illustrations or **visuals** made using computer software, showing how the outcome relates to its surroundings or a specific site or location.

Presentation using electronic and digital media

If you are working in graphics, video, film and digital photography, you might choose to present your outcomes or realisations on a CD or using a computer program such as PowerPoint. You should support work presented in this way with a digital or electronic sketchbook, a file, journal, workbook or sketchbook, which shows the investigation and development of your work.

Being selective in presentation

In presenting the Portfolio of Work you will need to carefully select, organise and present work that shows what you have carried out during the course. Careful selection and organisation are important if the presentation of your work is to be clear and effective in demonstrating how you have addressed each of the assessment objectives and have made an informed, meaningful and personal response in your work.

In the presentation of your work for the Externally Set Task, you might also need to be selective, not necessarily including every study or every image that you produce. Select what you need and consider the quality of your work rather than its quantity.

If you are mounting work, aim to keep the layout of studies and images neutral. If images are positioned poorly on a mount, either by the way that one image relates to another or because the arrangement of studies is at 'jaunty' angles, these can distract attention from the artwork. Poor quality, untidy or inappropriately decorative hand lettering or handwriting, a badly chosen typeface or font, can spoil the presentation of your work. A poorly considered presentation or layout can make connections between elements of your work less than clear.

Key terms

Mock-up: an assembled image or object to show how a design might look.

Visuals: visualisations or 'mock-ups' using a photo-montage technique to show, for example, how a large sculpture or construction might look in a landscape, a built environment or a public space.

CO links

See Chapter 1 for more about using digital and electronic media in developing ideas.

See Chapter 2 for more about experimenting with digital and electronic media.

See Chapter 3 for more ideas about using digital and electronic media for recording.

AQA Examiner's tip

Carefully select, organise and present your work.

Learning outcomes

Having read this chapter you should now be able to:

present a personal, informed and meaningful response

present your work to show the journey of your investigations and ideas

realise your intentions in the most appropriate way

make connections between the different aspects of your work, between visual, written, oral or other elements

respond critically to ideas, subjects, themes, briefs and issues in your own way

present your work effectively and in ways that are appropriate.

Case study references

Students

Abigail: *Case study* **19**
Endorsement: **Photography**
Area of study: **Light-based media**
Theme: **Identity; Issues based study**

Acheson: *Case studies* **23, 24, 32, 34**
Endorsement: **Graphic Communication**
Area of study: **Illustration**
Theme: **Distortion; Objects**

Daniel: *Case studies* **40, 45**
Endorsement: **Graphic Communication**
Area of study: **Corporate graphics**
Theme: **Responding to a brief**

Elizabeth: *Case studies* **21, 26, 30**
Endorsement: **Photography**
Area of study: **Lens- and light-based media**
Theme: **Detail; Environments**

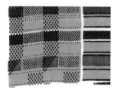

Isobel: *Case study* **20**
Endorsement: **Textile Design**
Area of study: **Print, dyeing and stitch**
Theme: **Cultural; Traditions**

Isobelle: *Case study* **17**
Endorsement: **Textile Design**
Area of study: **Mixed media**
Theme: **Environments**

Jake: *Case studies* **38, 43**
Endorsement: **Three-Dimensional Design**
Area of study: **Ceramics**
Theme: **Abstract; Decoration**

Jennifer: *Case study* **15**
Endorsement: **Art and Design**
Area of study: **Fine Art**
Theme: **Objects**

Jessica: *Case studies* **41, 42**
Endorsement: **Applied Art**
Area of study: **Graphic Communication**
Theme: **Responding to a brief**

Josh 1: *Case studies* **3, 12**
Endorsement: **Art and Design**
Area of study: **Three-Dimensional Design**
Theme: **The figure; The Body**

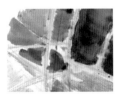

Josh 2: *Case studies* **4, 11**
Endorsement: **Art and Design**
Area of study: **Fine Art**
Theme: **Movement**

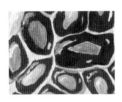

Kate: *Case study* **29**
Endorsement: **Art and Design**
Area of study: **Fine Art**
Theme: **Objects; Natural forms**

Katharine: *Case studies* **36, 39, 44**
Endorsement: **Fine Art**
Area of study: **Painting and drawing**
Theme: **Environments; Figures; Identity**

Kathryn: *Case study* **2**
Endorsement: **Art and Design**
Area of study: **Mixed media**
Theme: **Identity; 'Memories'**

Kirsty: *Case study* **18**
Endorsement: **Graphic Communication**
Area of study: **Illustration**
Theme: **Issues based study**

Lauren 1: *Case studies* **1, 5, 9**
Endorsement: **Fine Art**
Area of study: **Mixed media**
Theme: **Environments**

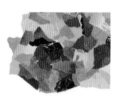

Lauren 2: *Case study* **14**
Endorsement: **Fine Art**
Area of study: **Mixed media**
Theme: **Objects**

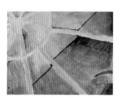

Lisa: *Case studies* **28, 33**
Endorsement: **Fine Art**
Area of study: **Painting and drawing**
Theme: **Objects**

Luke: *Case study* **27**
Endorsement: **Three-Dimensional Design**
Area of study: **Ceramics**
Theme: **Identity; Portraits**

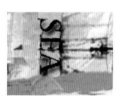

Nicole: *Case studies* **7, 10**
Endorsement: **Applied Art**
Area of study: **Graphic Communication**
Theme: **Responding to a brief**

Artists and designers

Air: *Case studies* **22, 25, 31**
Endorsement: **Graphic Communication**
Area of study: **Corporate graphics**
Theme: **Responding to a brief**
www.air-cs.co.uk

Amy Houghton: *Case studies* **6, 8, 13**
Endorsement: **Textile Design**
Area of study: **Mixed media**
Theme: **Objects**
www.amyhoughton.co.uk

Ian Murphy: *Case studies* **35, 37**
Endorsement: **Fine Art**
Area of study: **Drawing and painting**
Theme: **Environment**
www.ianmurphyartist.com

Sarah McCormack: *Case study* **16**
Endorsement: **Three-Dimensional Design**
Area of study: **Ceramics**
Theme: **Objects**
www.sarahmccormackceramics.homestead.com

Glossary

A

abstract: art that slightly, partially or completely departs from representing reality.

analytical studies: studies that analyse source material in depth.

area of study: painting, sculpture, printed textiles, ceramics, illustration, packaging design, film, for instance.

B

batik: the application of hot wax to a surface prior to colouring with dye. Successive additions of wax and dye can be built up to create a richly coloured piece.

biscuit firing: is the first stage in firing finished clay work. The dried clay is kiln fired to a high temperature, which creates a change in hardness, colour and surface and prepares the ceramic piece for the application of coloured glazes.

bitumen: a product extracted from oil.

C

ceramic: is the term used to describe art work made in clay. The word is derived from the Greek word 'keramos' meaning pottery.

collage: a technique for creating images by pasting together fragments of 2D and 3D materials.

collagraph: a print produced by inking an image block created from pieced cardboard, paper, string, etc.

colourway: a range of colour combinations for a design, layout, fabric or pattern.

composition: the arrangement of lines, shapes, forms and spaces in relation to each other.

contextual sources: examples of art, craft and design, cultural objects, artefacts, including architecture from different times and cultures.

critical understanding: responding in an informed way that shows appropriateness and understanding in developing your work and realising your intentions, and in responding to the work of others.

cross-hatching: shading by intersecting parallel lines.

D

design brief: developing ideas with a defined focus, particularly in Graphic Communication, Three-Dimensional Design, Textile Design and Applied Art.

design sheet: a sheet of studies that demonstrates or presents the development of an idea, sometimes in a logical sequence or progression of images, sometimes showing the exploration of alternative ideas.

digital media: digital cameras, video, camcorders and sound recording equipment.

drypoint: the production of a print by scratching an image into an acrylic or soft metal plate with a sharp tool. The plate is then inked and printed.

E

electronic media: computers, scanners, printers and photocopiers.

evaluate: to look back, reflecting on the strengths and weaknesses of an idea or image, comparing ideas or images and making a judgement or decision.

F

figurative: recognisable representations of the human figure, animals, objects and places.

formal elements: the building blocks of art and design – line, shape, tone, texture, colour and form. These are often referred to as 'visual elements'.

format: the type of layout and presentation of an image or design work, for example, whether it is 'portrait' or 'landscape', or how it is folded.

frottage: the transfer of a relief image or surface by placing a sheet of paper over the design and rubbing it firmly with crayon, chalk or charcoal.

G

gesso: a type of white plaster which is applied to a surface to provide a ground for painting.

glaze: is a decorative coating used on pottery or ceramic sculpture. It can be applied by dipping, spraying or direct painting of the vessel. Glazed work is fired to a high temperature to fix the coating.

gouache: an opaque paint which can be mixed with water and applied to a surface to give a flat, smooth and dense colour.

I

illusion: the creation of a deceptive appearance. For example, the illusion of a 3-D object drawn on a flat sheet of paper.

J

journal: a collection of information about technical data, techniques and processes, and reflections on contextual material relevant to the development of your work.

L

layout: for example, the arrangement of images on

a mount or study sheet, the arrangement of images and typography on a page.

log: a diary, both written and visual that usually relates to an event or experience such as a workshop or gallery visit.

logo: a logo is a distinctive sign or symbol that identifies a product, company or agency.

M

maquette: a small 3D study or model, usually to scale, that explores shape, form and space, often translated from drawings. A maquette is like a 3D working drawing.

media: the materials used to create a piece of art work such as pencil, paint, oil pastel, charcoal, chalk, pen and ink, fabric, clay.

mind map: a method of exploring thoughts and insights, and generating possible ideas quickly, often in written form – sometimes known as 'word storming', or a 'spider diagram'.

mock-up: an assembled image or object to show how a design might look.

mood board: usually in the form of collage, photo-montage or collected materials, the mood-board is often used in textiles and interior design to explore initial ideas about colour, tone and texture.

O

over-painting: applying repeated layers of paint to a surface. The paint can be allowed to dry before each layer is applied or subsequent layers may be built up in different paint consistencies or with different brush sizes to create a sense of texture.

P

photogram: a photograph produced by using an object instead of a negative in the darkroom. A method used by Louis Daguerre and Man Ray.

pictorial elements: the component parts of a composition. For example trees, fields, buildings and sky are the visual elements of a rural landscape.

pictorial: the representation of space and depth. The illusion of three-dimensions in landscape painting or photography, for example.

plan: a drawing or diagram showing layout, arrangement or structure of something.

primary sources: source material that you can study directly from first-hand experience, for example a still-life group in the art room, a performance, working in a landscape or from a painting in a gallery.

R

reflect: to look back at your work and think about how it has progressed, in relation to your intentions.

S

sampler: in Textile Design, a small working study that shows what a finished constructed or printed textile will look like.

screen grab: a way of saving images to show the stages of development in your work.

secondary sources: reproductions of images and artefacts, music, text, poetry, film – source material that is produced by others.

sgraffito: a method of creating a design on a surface by scratching through an upper layer of colour to reveal the colour or surface beneath. It is a technique often used in ceramics.

source material: objects, artefacts and images, including texts or performances, that inform your work.

source materials: materials such as objects, artefacts and images from which you develop your work and ideas. They might include texts, poetry, writing, sound, music, TV and film.

starting point: a theme, object, issue or brief.

T

typeface: different styles of type. Also referred to as 'fonts', especially in connection with computers.

typography: the design of typefaces, and the layout of type.

V

visual language: the ways that we use visual elements such as line, tone, colour and form, in a personal way.

visuals: visualisations or 'mock-ups' using a photo-montage technique to show, for example, how a large sculpture or construction might look in a landscape, a built environment or a public space.

W

wash: a thin mix of watercolour paint and water.

weight: creating the impression that something is heavy.

Index

Note: key terms are in **bold**